THE
JEWELRY
MAKING
HANDBOOK

D0326145

THE
JEWELRY
MAKING
HANDBOOK

Simple techniques and step-by-step projects

Sharon McSwiney
Penny Williams
Claire C Davies
Jennie Davies

CHARTWELL
BOOKS, INC.

This edition published in 2007 by
Chartwell Books, Inc.
A division of Book Sales Inc.
114 Northfield Avenue
Edison, New Jersey 08837
USA

ISBN-13: 978-0-7858-2299-8
ISBN-10: 0-7858-2299-2

A Quintet Book
Copyright © 2007 Quintet Publishing Limited
All rights reserved

No part of this publication may be reproduced,
stored in a retrieval system, or transmitted in any
form or by any means, electronic, mechanical,
photocopying, recording or otherwise, without the
prior written permission of the copyright holder.

This book was designed and produced by
Quintet Publishing Limited
6 Blundell Street
London N7 9BH, UK

Art Director: Simon Thompson
Photography: Paul Forrester
Editors: Anne Johnson, Jo Silman
Senior Editor: Marian Broderick
Publisher: Gaynor Sermon

The material in this publication previously
appeared in *The Creative Jeweller.*
Every effort has been made to obtain copyright
clearance, and we apologize for any omissions.

Printed in China by
Midas Printing International Limited

9 8 7 6 5 4 3 2 1

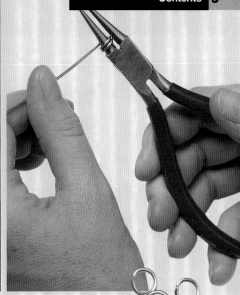

Contents

Introduction

Jewelry is often considered to be an expensive accessory. This book sets out to explain in simple steps how to produce stylish and modern necklaces, bracelets, brooches, and earrings that are individual and expressive in design, while also developing basic skills in the art of jewelry-making. A wealth of inspirational projects offer the reader an ideal introduction to the creation of modern pieces.

All of the projects are laid out in easy-to-follow steps, illustrated with helpful demonstration photographs. A wide spectrum of processes use materials ranging from precious metals to everyday "found" objects and recycled paper. Techniques such as beadwork, wirework, and metal-forming are used to create exciting and innovative designs. The projects also vary in complexity, so that the maker can develop confidence while mastering a variety of skills from the straightforward to the complex.

The dictionary defines jewelry as "any item worn or used for adornment." This book illustrates that jewelry does not have to be made from precious metal and gemstones, or require lots of specialist equipment. Jewelry can be made from a whole host of materials. It can be fun or even ephemeral. In the past, earrings,

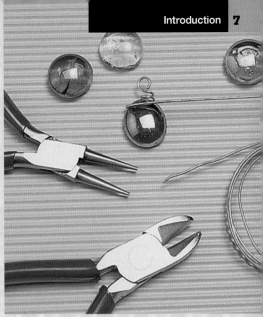

brooches, and necklaces have been created from hair, bone, coal, or glass. In some cultures, natural resources such as seeds, feathers, clay, animal skulls, and bones are used.

Throughout history, old or unfashionable jewelry has been reset in the current style—and the theme of recycling is a key element in some of the projects in this book. Modern recycling includes the use of aluminum cans, telephone wire, and bottle tops in the creation of new jewelery design.

As well as new and recycled material, jewelry can be made from "found" objects. These could be items that evoke memories of past events, or things collected from nature that inspire you.

Some techniques in jewelry-making do require highly specialist and expensive equipment; however, with the basic tools and materials, plus the help of the easy-to-follow projects set out in this book, it is possible to create pieces of jewelry that are both innovatively designed and professional in appearance, yet can be worn on any occasion.

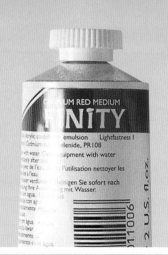

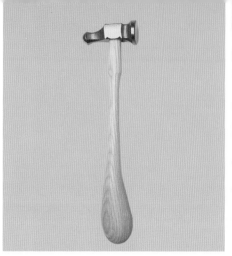

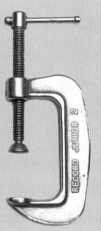

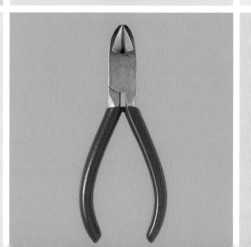

Materials, tools, and equipment

The following pages show that there is a huge variety of materials to choose from when making jewelry, from base metals to modern rubber to modeling clay. After that, you can let your imagination run wild, decorating unique bracelets, necklaces, and earrings with a vast and inexpensive range of colorful paints, glass beads, glittery sequins—and fun "found" objects, such as shells. Your basic set of tools and equipment should include pliers, files, wire wool, and tin snips. But as your confidence grows, you will create more advanced pieces, using hammers, drills, and center punches.

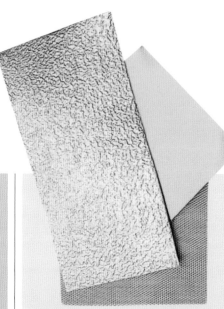

Thick linen thread

Available in a range of neutral colors, thick linen thread complements natural beads. It is easy to knot and so creates a good base structure for threading beads. It can be purchased waxed and unwaxed. Waxed thread has a protective coating that makes it durable and creates a sheen on the surface of the thread, which adds to the effect of the jewelry.

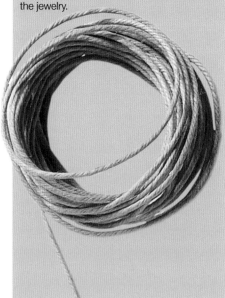

Sheet metal

The metals most commonly used in jewelry-making can be split into two main groups: non-ferrous metals, such as copper, brass, tin, and aluminum, or precious metals, such as silver and gold.

Copper
Pinkish red in color, malleable, and easy to work with, copper is readily available in both sheet and wire form.

Brass
Pale yellow in color, brass is a harder metal than copper.

Sterling silver
Softer than copper or brass, sterling silver contains 925 parts in 1000 of fine silver. It is available from specialist refiners or bullion dealers, most of whom allow you to purchase small quantities at a time. You can often select from offcuts, or you can have pieces cut to a specific size.

Self-hardening clay

This clay substance hardens on contact with air and therefore requires no baking or firing. It is available in terracotta or white from many art and craft stores.

Inks and enamels

Enamel paint

Many different colors are produced in both matt and transparent varieties. Available in small pots from hardware, model, or craft stores, enamel paint requires 4 to 6 hours of drying time. Clean the brushes you have used with enamel thinners.

Inks

Water-based inks are used for coloring and staining a variety of surfaces, and can be bought in small pots from art or stationery stores. Inks come in a wide range of colors, including gold and silver. They can be used as a wood stain or as an alternative to paint.

Leather thong

Available in a range of thicknesses and colors, leather thong is flexible, durable, and strong. This makes it easy to knot and to thread quantities of beads without fear of the thong breaking. It also works well in contrast to lengths of metal tubing and metallic beads.

Findings

This is the term applied to the small components used in jewelry-making, such as earring clips, stems or posts, and backs. Findings can be bought ready-made from specialist suppliers or craft stores, and are available in precious and plated base metal forms. Jump rings are the small rings of wire that are often used to link components together and attach earring hooks.

Modeling plastic

Available in strips and blocks, this comes in various colors and finishes and is obtainable from art and craft stores.

Cabochon and faceted glass stones

These stones are flat-backed and foiled to create highly reflective surfaces that give a jewel-like quality. They can easily be set into a self-hardening modeling clay.

Oven-baked clay

A plastic modeling material that is baked in the oven to harden, this clay is sold in small blocks in most art and craft stores. There are numerous colors available.

Paints

Gouache and acrylic paints can both be used to decorate paper and cardboard-based projects.

Gouache paint

A good quality poster paint, gouache is sold in art stores. Available in tubes or pots in a wide spectrum of colors, it is water-soluble and dries quickly.

Acrylic paint

Obtainable from art stores in either pot or tubes, acrylic comes in a very wide variety of colors. Like gouache, acrylic is water-soluble and can be used on paper projects as an alternative to the more metallic enamel paints.

Beads
and sequins

Thousands of bead variations from different
countries in innumerable sizes, shapes, and
colors are available. They are most often
made from ceramics, glass, plastic, metal, or
wood. Most craft stores will stock beads—
and there are even stores specializing only
in beads.

Rubber tube

Easy to cut, rubber tube can be found in
most car accessory stores, and it makes
simple yet effective parts for jewelry.

Thick silk ribbon

Available in a variety of widths, colors, and textures, thick silk ribbon is excellent to use when creating close-fitting chokers.

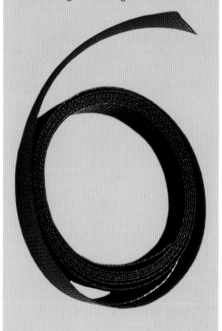

Newspaper

Utilize the versatility of paper and recycle old newspapers to create durable, wearable, individual necklaces.

Silver, brass, and copper wire

Metal wire comes in a variety of thicknesses. It is usually sold in a softened or annealed state so that it is easy to manipulate.

Glitter pens

These pens, available from good stationery stores, contain ready-mixed glue and glitter. They can be used as an alternative to paints. Always read the instructions to ensure that you cause no damage to fabrics and plastics.

Hammers

Chasing hammer
With a polished flat surface on one end and a ball shape on the other, this hammer is useful for flattening or texturing metal. A ball pein hammer is less expensive than the chasing hammer, but used in the same way.

Nylon mallet
This tool is essential if you want to flatten metal without marking the surface.

Metal scriber

A hardened steel rod, tapered to a sharp point, used to score lines into metal surfaces. These lines can be functional, such as one to follow when cutting, or simply decorative.

Adhesives

Resin-based glue (epoxy)
A strong bonding glue that requires the mixing of an adhesive and hardener to enable it to work, it is available in tube form or in a syringe. Follow manufacturers' instructions.

All purpose, clear, strong adhesive
Useful for sticking non-metal items such as wood, fabric, and some plastics together, it is available in tubes. Use in a well-ventilated area.

PVA
A white, non-toxic, water-based glue, it is particularly suitable for bonding paper, card, and fabrics. Available in tubes or plastic bottles, it can be applied with a brush. Rinse the brush under water immediately after use.

Files

Files are used to remove unwanted burrs or blemishes on the edges of metal surfaces, to enlarge holes, or bevel edges. Various types are available, with small needle files being particularly useful. There are also different shapes and cuts, 00 being the coarsest and 6 the finest. The teeth on a file only cut on the forward stroke, therefore the file should be lifted on the backward stroke so that it is not in contact with the metal.

Wire cutters

They come in a variety of sizes depending on the thickness of wire to be cut. Occasionally wire cutters are incorporated within a pair of pliers.

Jeweler's piercing saw

This saw is used for cutting all types of sheet metal. Different size blades are available for cutting different thicknesses of metal.

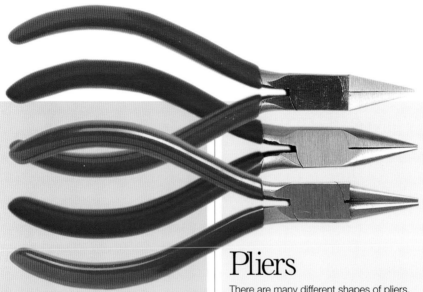

Pliers

There are many different shapes of pliers, the most commonly used being (see above, from top to bottom) flat-nosed, half-round, and round-nosed. They are used for shaping, curling, bending, and flattening wire.

Wire wool

Used for cleaning the surface of sheet metal, it removes grease and dirt, leaving a satin finish.

Center punch

The center punch is a rod of steel with a point on the end and is used to make an indentation in metal before drilling a hole. Sometimes it is used to punch a texture.

Drill

Special jeweler's hand drills are available, but a small general purpose drill from hardware stores is perfectly adequate to make holes in different materials, provided the chuck holds small-size drill bits. The most useful sizes of drill bits are $1/32$ in/0.8 mm and $3/32$ in/2.4 mm.

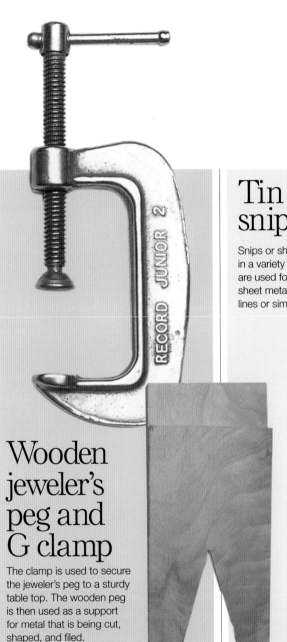

Tin snips

Snips or shears come in a variety of sizes and are used for cutting flat sheet metal in straight lines or simple curves.

Wooden jeweler's peg and G clamp

The clamp is used to secure the jeweler's peg to a sturdy table top. The wooden peg is then used as a support for metal that is being cut, shaped, and filed.

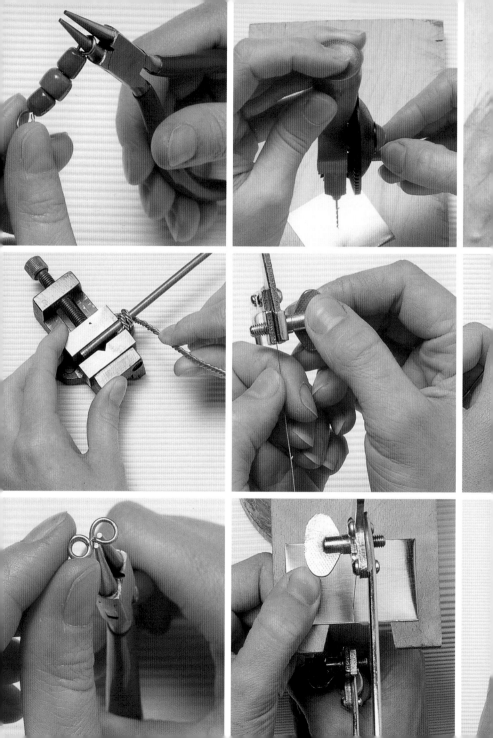

Techniques

The basic techniques used in the projects are explained in this section from how to create exciting metal shapes to how to make your own fasteners. Ready-made fasteners can be bought from most jewelry suppliers but, because the findings (see page 12) are quite simple, making them yourself means they can become an integral part of your design.

A thin copper or brass sheet can be textured easily to make a brooch (see page 88).

Hammering

Metal
You can create texture by hammering a metal surface. Hold the hammer handle with a firm grip toward the end, with the index finger extended along the handle for support. Do not "batter" the metal but apply rhythmic taps.

Nylon mallet
Hammering with a nylon mallet flattens sheet metal or wire, without affecting the surface.

Drilling

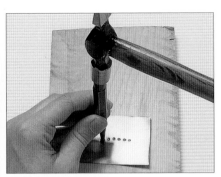

Center punch
You can use a center punch to create decorative punched dots on a metal surface. Hold the punch vertically to the metal and lightly tap the top with a flat-sided hammer.

1 Before drilling a metal surface, it is important to center-punch the place where you want the hole to be. This will prevent the drill from skating over the surface and give it a precise starting point.

Wire
Hammering wire flattens, textures, and hardens it. The wire therefore keeps its form better.

2 Hold the drill in a vertical position. Start to turn the handle slowly to enable the drill bit to bite, but do not put any pressure on the drill or the drill bit may break.

Sawing metal

1 Use a piercing saw frame and a blade. Blades come in a variety of sizes depending on the metal you need to cut. Make sure the blade has the rough side pointing out from the frame and the teeth pointing down toward the ground. Open the nut and bolt at the top of the frame. Trap the blade in the gap provided and screw it back together as tightly as possible.

2 Prop the saw frame into the peg. Lower the other end of the blade between the other nut and bolt. Push your weight against the frame while tightening the blade in position. Release the weight and the blade should be held in position under tension. If there is any movement in the blade, it is not tight enough.

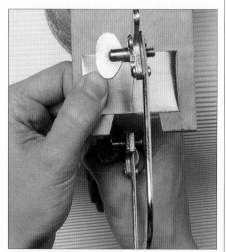

3 Hold the metal firmly over the peg. Keeping the saw at a 90-degree angle to the ground, gently move it forward. The saw will only cut on the down stroke. Do not push too hard because the thin blades break very easily. Take your time to master using the saw.

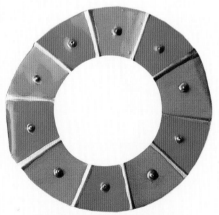

You can achieve a variety of shapes by using metal sheeting (see page 92).

Cutting shapes

1 Make a center-punch mark on the metal at the edge of the shape you need to cut.

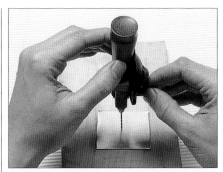

2 Drill a small hole through the center punch mark, large enough for the piercing blade to fit through.

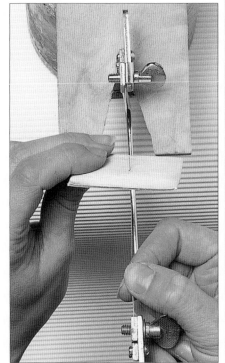

3 Open one end of the piercing saw and thread the blade through the hole. Tighten up the blade again.

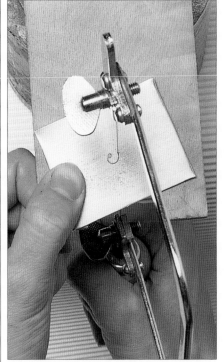

4 Hold the metal firmly against the peg and cut out the desired shape.

Jump rings

1 Cut a 6-in/15-cm length of wire, secure one end in a pair of round-nosed pliers, and slowly bend the wire around one side of the pliers to create the beginning of a coil.

2 Continue to coil the wire around the pliers until all of the wire is used and a regular coil of wire is formed.

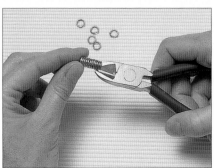

3 Remove the coil from the pliers and, using a pair of wire snips, cut up one side of the coil.

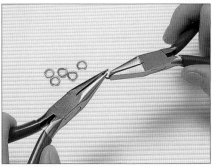

4 The jump rings can be opened using two pairs of flat-nosed pliers; another jump ring can then be threaded on, and the host jump ring closed.

5 You can create a chain by repeating the process of linking jump rings together.

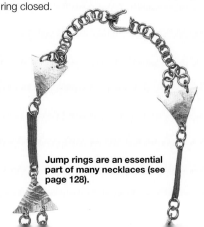

Jump rings are an essential part of many necklaces (see page 128).

Bead wires

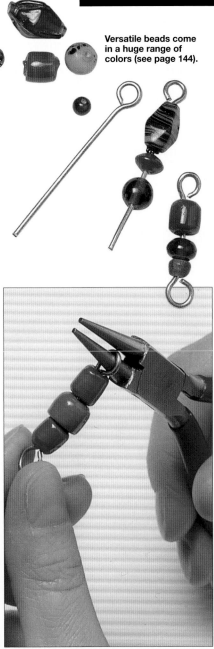

Versatile beads come in a huge range of colors (see page 144).

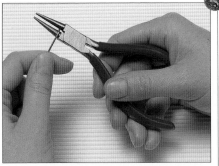

1 Assemble the beads to be threaded and assess what length they will be. Cut a length of wire about 1 in/2.5 cm longer than the length of beads to be threaded.

2 Secure one end of the wire using round-nosed pliers and bend it to create a loop.

3 Thread the beads onto the wire, pushing them up to the looped end of the wire.

4 Secure the beads by bending the remaining wire into a loop with the pliers.

Twisting wire

1 Cut two 48-in/120-cm lengths of wire and bend them in half. Secure the ends in a vise. Take a hooked wire fastened into a drill, and hook it onto the looped end of the bent wires.

2 Turn the hand drill to make the wires twist together. It is important to turn the drill slowly to allow the wires to twist together evenly.

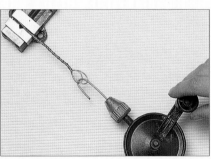

3 Continue to turn the drill until the wires are twisted together along the length of the wire, at the desired looseness or tightness.

4 Remove the twisted wires from the vise and drill. Using the wire snips, cut off the looped end, so you are left with an even length of wire.

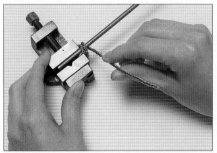

5 Secure a circular rod and one end of the twisted wire in a vise. Slowly bend the twisted wire around the rod.

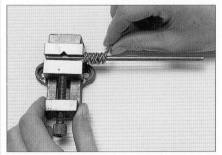

6 Continue to bend the twisted wire around the rod until all of the wire has been used and the wires have formed a coil.

Fastener for thong

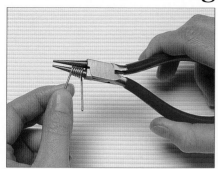

1 With wire snips, cut a piece of wire 10 in/25 cm. Use the round-nosed pliers to grip one end of the wire and coil it around one side of the pliers, from the bottom and coiling upward.

2 When you have an even coil, remove the coiled wire from the pliers by slipping it over the end of the nose.

3 Use the round-nosed pliers to bend the end lengths of wire into either a loop or a hook; this will become the actual fastening.

4 To attach the leather thong to the coiled wire fastening, thread the thong through the center of the coil. Tie a knot in the end of the thong and pull the thong back so that the knot is discreetly hidden inside of the coil.

5 Finish the fastening by trimming off the excess thong using a pair of scissors.

Instead of making a fastener, you can tie a knot in a thong (see page 152).

Coiled loop fastener

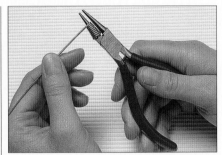

1 Cut a piece of wire approximately 10 in/25 cm in length. Using a pair of round-nosed pliers, coil the wire, starting from the bottom of the pliers and working upward.

2 Continue to coil the wire along the length of the nose of the pliers, keeping the growing coil tight and even.

3 Remove the tapering coil from the pliers and use the excess straight wire to form a loop.

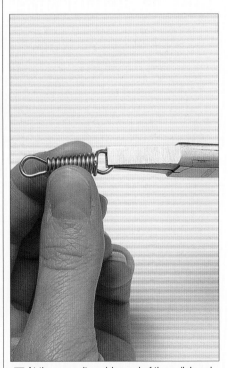

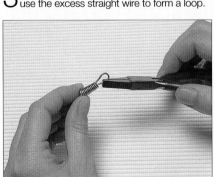

4 The loop is created by bending the wire over on itself and tucking the end into the coil. This forms the fastening mechanism.

5 At the opposite, wider end of the coil, bend the last coil in half at 90 degrees, making sure the end of the wire is tucked into the coil. This is where fastener and necklace connect.

Single wire loop fastener

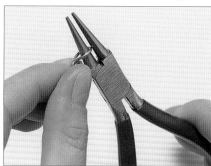

1 Cut a length of wire approximately 9 in/22 cm in length. Use the round-nosed pliers to coil the wire around one and a half times.

2 Holding the coils between your fingers, bend the wire in a large loop with the aid of the round-nosed pliers.

3 To finish the fastener, cut the wire where the loop comes around full circle. Make sure this loop is larger than the first coil to ensure easy fastening.

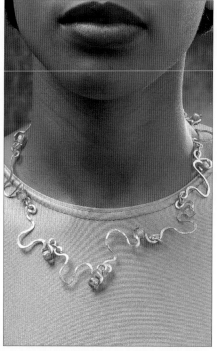

Many lightweight necklaces, such as this silver-wire and bead version (see page 67), can be safely secured using a delicate single wire loop and hook fastener.

Coiled hook fastener

1 Cut a length of wire approximately 12 in/30 cm in length. Using a pair of round-nosed pliers, coil the wire, starting from the bottom of the pliers and working upward.

2 Using the flat-nosed pliers, bend the excess wire at 90 degrees. With the round-nosed pliers, bend the wire over, forming a loop.

3 Using the tips of the round-nosed pliers, bend the wire back on itself, forming a hook.

4 With the flat-nosed pliers manipulate the bent back wire so that it follows the first wire.

5 When the wire is bent, cut off excess wire with wire snips and tuck the end into the coil. Switch to the flat-nosed pliers.

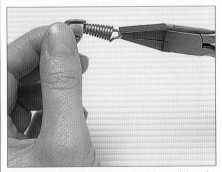

6 At the opposite, wider end of the coil, bend the last coil in half at 90 degrees, making sure the end of the wire is tucked into the coil. This is where fastener and necklace connect.

Single wire hook fastener

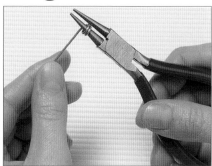

1 Cut a length of wire approximately 9 in/22 cm in length. Use the round-nosed pliers to coil the wire around one and a half times.

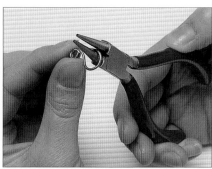

2 Holding the coils between your fingers, bend the wire in a large loop with the aid of the round-nosed pliers.

Heavier neckpieces (see page 144) need secure fastenings, such as coiled hooks and loops.

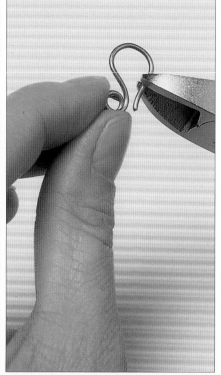

3 To finish the hook fastening, cut off the excess wire with the wire snips.

Wire

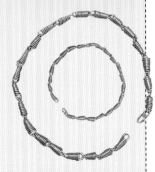

Spiraled silver choker

Quantities of silver wire are coiled tightly to make a chunky, close-fitting necklace with a richly textured surface quality.

YOU WILL NEED...

* ruler
* wire snips
* 5 yards/4.5 meters of 14-gauge silver wire
* round-nosed pliers
* flat-nosed pliers

SEE ALSO...

* Coiled loop fastener p.34
* Coiled hook fastener p.36

1 Cut 22 lengths of wire, each measuring 6½ in/16 cm. Grip one end of one piece of silver wire in the pliers and wrap it around one side of the tapering nose, starting at the bottom of the pliers and coiling upwards. Repeat on all lengths.

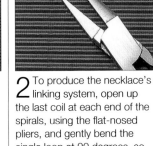

2 To produce the necklace's linking system, open up the last coil at each end of the spirals, using the flat-nosed pliers, and gently bend the single loop at 90 degrees, so that it sits at right angles to the body of the spiral. Repeat.

3 Line up the coiled wires in the final design, the narrow taper facing the widest end of the next coiled section. With the flat-nosed pliers, open the bent links and thread on the next coiled section. Close the link, making sure it is secure.

4 Link together all of the spirals until they are fastened to one another in a chain. Finish the necklace by making and attaching an integral coiled hook and loop fastening.

Spiral pin

Fine silver wire tightly bound around
stronger silver wire produces a pin that
is both decorative and durable.

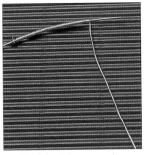

1 Bind the 14-gauge wire
around the 7-gauge wire.
Leave 2½ in/6 cm of 14-gauge
wire uncovered at one end and
¾ in/2 cm uncovered at the
other end.

2 Thread your bead onto the
shorter uncovered end of
the 14-gauge wire and bend
back the wire to secure. Cut
off any excess 7-gauge wire.

3 Begin to spiral the bound
wire around the bead. Curl
and twist the wire to produce
an aesthetically pleasing
form, until you get to within
½ in/1 cm of the uncovered
14-gauge wire.

4 Turn the piece over. Curl
over the exposed 14-gauge
wire to form a pin, and use the
wire at the bead end to form a
hook. Cut off any excess wire
and file to a fine point.

YOU WILL NEED...

* 12 in/30 cm of 14-
  gauge silver wire

* 96 in/240 cm
  of 7-gauge silver wire

* one decorative bead

* wire cutters

* round-nosed pliers

* half-round pliers

* needle file

SEE ALSO...

* Twisting wire p.32

Sophisticated silver

A discreet but elegant modern necklace, contrasting the clean lines of silver tubing with a black leather thong.

1 With a pencil, mark off the silver tube into 17 separate lengths, each measuring 1⅜ in/3.5 cm. With a piercing saw, carefully cut the tube. File both ends of the cut sections with a needle file.

2 Tie a tight knot 1½ in/4 cm from one end of the black leather thong and thread on one section of the silver tube. Tie another knot close to the other end of the tube to secure it in place on the black leather thong. Repeat this process until all of the sections of tube have been used.

YOU WILL NEED...

* pencil
* 24 in/60 cm of 28-gauge silver tube
* ruler
* piercing saw frame and blades
* needle file
* 32 in/80 cm of fine black leather thong
* scissors

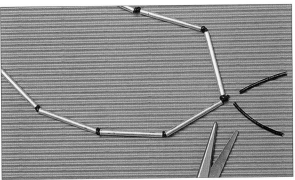

3 To finish, tie the two ends of the thong together securely. Finally, cut off any excess lengths of thong.

SEE ALSO...
* Sawing metal p.28

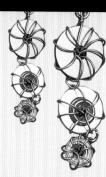

Drop earrings

Ordinary household washers are wrapped with fine wire and linked together to produce attractive drop earrings.

YOU WILL NEED...

* ruler

* wire cutters

* 54 in/137 cm of 10-gauge brass wire

* two ¾-in/2-cm diameter (¼-in/5-mm center hole) washers

* half-round pliers

* two ⅞-in/2.2.cm diameter (⅜-in/1 cm center hole) washers

* four No. 6 screw cup brass washers

* six jump rings

* two earring hooks

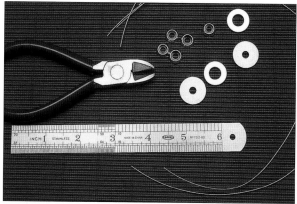

1 Cut the following lengths of wire: two 12-in/30-cm lengths, two 8-in/20-cm lengths, two 7-in/18-cm lengths.

2 Starting with the ¾-in/2-cm washer, thread a 12-in/30-cm length of wire through the central hole and bind it around the washer. Twist the excess wire at the starting point and curl around to form a loop. Repeat with the other ¾-in/2-cm washer.

3 Wrap a ⅞-in/2.2-cm washer with an 8-in/20-cm length of wire, which also holds a screw cup washer. Tuck the ends of the wire into the middle hole. Repeat.

4 Finally, bind a 7-in/18-cm length of wire around each of the remaining screw cup washers.

5 Link the three sections together with jump rings.

6 Attach an earring hook to the top twisted loop of wire to complete the earrings.

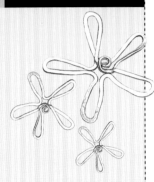

Silver wire flowers

Silver is a material that is easy to manipulate, but for contrasting color effects, experiment with metals, such as copper or brass wire.

YOU WILL NEED...

∗ ruler

∗ wire cutters

∗ 28 in/70 cm of 14-gauge round section sterling silver wire

∗ 8 in/20 cm of 10-gauge round section sterling silver wire

∗ round-nosed pliers

∗ hammer

∗ flat needle file

∗ four silver jump rings

SEE ALSO...

∗ Findings p.12
∗ Hammering p.26
∗ Jump rings p.30
∗ Twisting wire p.32

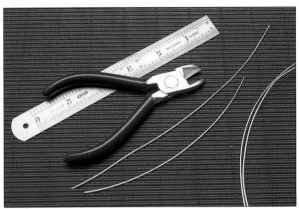

1 Measure and cut the following: two 8-in/20-cm lengths and two 6-in/15-cm lengths of 14-gauge silver wire, two 4-in/10-cm lengths of 10-gauge silver wire.

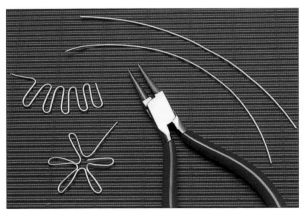

2 Using round-nosed pliers, form the 14-gauge wire pieces into a zigzag pattern. Bend the wire around to form the "petals." Leave ½ in/1.2 cm of wire unformed on the end of each flower.

3 When complete, hammer the flowers to flatten and slightly texture their surface.

4 With round-nosed pliers, form a central spiral in each flower from the remaining ½ in/1 cm of wire.

5 Using the 10-gauge lengths of wire, form spirals, leaving 1 in/2.5 cm unformed. Hammer the spirals flat. Then, bend the remaining wire into a hook.

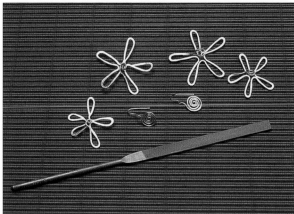

6 Using a flat needle file, file the ends of the hooks until they are smooth.

7 Assemble the earrings using four jump rings, two for each earring, to connect the flowers and hooks.

Folded brass and glass

This simple yet bold design uses brass wire contrasted with black beads to create a rhythmic folded wire necklace.

YOU WILL NEED...

* ruler

* wire snips

* 4 yards/3.5 meters of 14-gauge brass wire

* round-nosed pliers

* hammer

* protective gloves

* ten flat round glass beads

* two pairs flat-nosed pliers

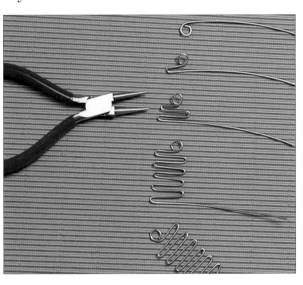

SEE ALSO...

* Hammering p.26
* Bead wires p.31

1 With the wire snips, cut ten 12-in/30-cm lengths of brass wire. Using a pair of round-nosed pliers, make connecting loops on each end of each length of wire. Take the pliers and bend the wire back and forth on itself to produce an undulating pattern 1 in/2.5 cm wide. Repeat the process until nearly all of the wire has been used.

2 Wearing protective gloves and using a hammer, tap the wires gently on a firm surface to flatten them.

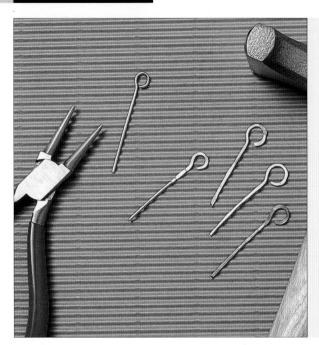

3 Using wire snips, cut ten 1-in/2.5-cm lengths of brass wire. Using the round-nosed pliers, make a loop at one end of the wire. Using the hammer, gently tap the looped wires on a firm surface to flatten them.

4 Thread a glass bead onto each short wire and, with a pair of round-nosed pliers, make a loop at the other end of the wire to secure the bead.

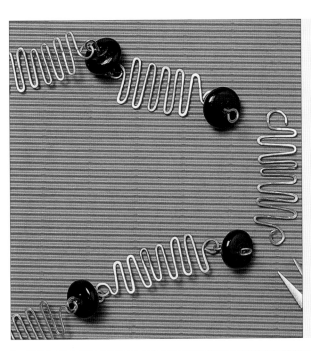

5 Using two pairs of flat-nosed pliers, open up the loops of all the sections and connect the loops together, in the sequence shown, to form the necklace.

6 Close the loops with the flat-nosed pliers, making sure that all of the linked loops are securely fastened together.

Fantasy bird

This striking yet elegant silver wire pin is inspired by the beautiful and exotic birdlife of South America.

YOU WILL NEED...

* 32 in/80 cm of 14-gauge silver wire

* half-round pliers

* round-nosed pliers

* wire cutters

* 36 in/90 cm of 7-gauge silver wire

* one ⅛-in/3-mm blue glass bead

* five ⅛-in/3-mm silver-plated beads

* needle file

* pin stopper

1 Using the round-nosed pliers, bend the 14-gauge silver wire into the body of a bird, working toward the tail, and leaving a pin 3 in/7.5 cm long at one end.

2 Complete the shape of your bird and cut off any excess wire.

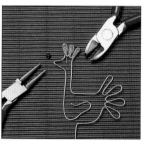

3 Bind some of the 7-gauge wire around the comb of the bird. Leave enough wire to thread on and secure the blue glass bead just above the beak, to make an eye.

4 Bind the rest of the 7-gauge wire around the tail feathers, leaving spare ends of wire at the tail tips. Thread four of the silver beads onto the tail tips, then loop the wire to complete. Thread a bead onto the loop of the bird wing. Cut and file the pin and put the pin stopper on the end.

SEE ALSO...

* Bead wires p.31

Bobbin bead bracelet

This subtle and surprising bracelet is created by using a method that is traditionally reserved for weaving wool.

YOU WILL NEED...

* chunky piece of wood
* drill
* pen
* five miniature screws
* screwdriver
* coil of very fine metal wire
* metal beads or small colored glass beads
* flat-nosed pliers
* wire cutters
* two jump rings
* two fasteners

1 To make a bobbin, drill a hole approximately 2 in/5 cm in diameter through the piece of wood.

2 With a pen, evenly make five marks as shown. Where marked, securely screw in the five miniature screws. Your bobbin is now complete.

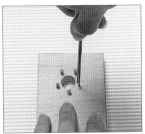

SEE ALSO...

* Drilling p.27
* Jump rings p.30
* Bead wires p.31

3 Thread approximately 25 beads onto your wire.

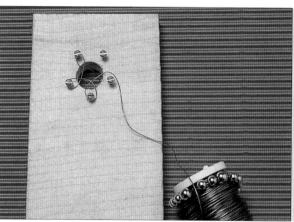

4 Loop the wire around your bobbin as shown.

5 Continue to loop your wire, lifting the lower loop up and over the top loop each time with your flat-nosed pliers.

6 Gradually add the beads, by sliding them down the wire while you continue to loop as before. Although the process is very slow, the results are rewarding and the finished product is delightful.

7 Your length of bracelet should emerge from the underside of the bobbin. Just continue looping and lifting, and adding the beads, until the bracelet is the length you desire. You could also make many lengths and fasten them to each other on the wrist.

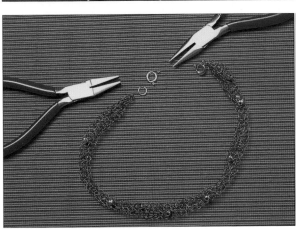

8 Secure a jump ring and fastener to each end, so they can be linked when you wear the bracelet.

Braided silver choker

In this simple and delicate design, fine silver wires are braided together to create a close-fitting neckpiece.

YOU WILL NEED...

✳ string

✳ ruler

✳ 3 yards/2.75 meters of 7-gauge silver wire

✳ wire snips

✳ vise

✳ round-nosed pliers

✳ two pairs flat-nosed pliers

1 Loosely place a length of string around the neck and measure its length. Add 2½ in/6 cm. Using the string as a guide, cut six lengths of the silver wire with wire snips.

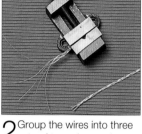

2 Group the wires into three sets of two wires and place the ends of all six wires securely in a vise. Braid these three sets until all of the wires are braided together.

3 Remove the wires from the vise and use two pairs of flat-nosed pliers to twist the ends of the braided wires together. To do this, hold the wires 1 in from the end with one pair of pliers and, using the other pair, slowly twist the ends together. Do this at both ends to secure the wires.

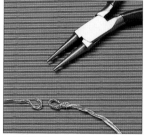

4 With the round-nosed pliers, bend one end around to form a hook. For the other end, take a longer length and bend it until it forms a loop. Twist any excess wires around the necklace, securing the loop in place. Flatten any sharp wires. Finally, bend the braided wires into a circle.

SEE ALSO...

✳ Twisting wire p.32

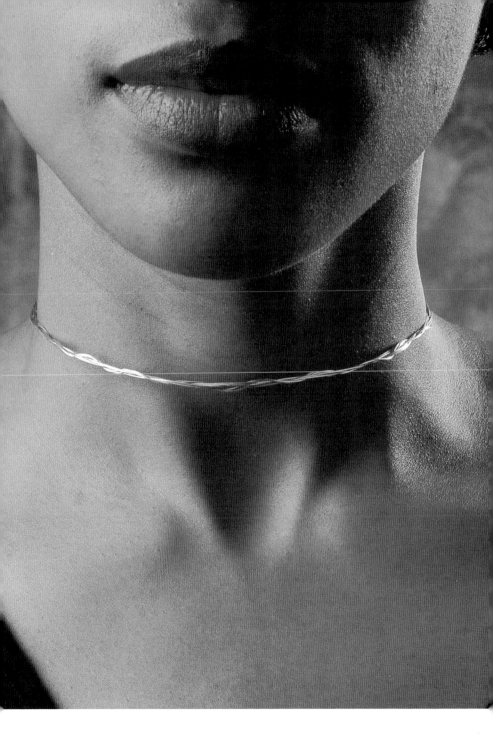

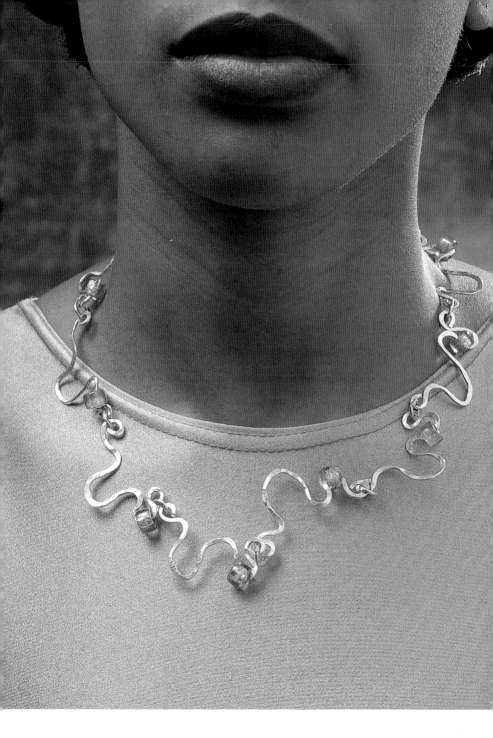

Textured silver

Substantial wire is manipulated in a lively manner and combined with gold glass beads to create a flamboyant necklace.

YOU WILL NEED...

* ✳ pencil
* ✳ paper
* ✳ ruler
* ✳ 45 in/115 cm of 18-gauge silver wire
* ✳ wire snips
* ✳ round-nosed pliers
* ✳ flat-nosed pliers
* ✳ hammer
* ✳ ten gold barrel glass beads
* ✳ coiled loop and hook fastening

1 With a pencil and a piece of paper, draw the undulating shape, 2½ in/6 cm long. Allow for a loop at both ends. This is the template for the wire components. Cut ten 2½-in/6-cm lengths of silver wire with wire snips. Using the round-nosed pliers, manipulate the wires to the shape of the paper template. Make a loop at one end of each wire with the pliers.

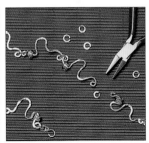

2 Hammer the wires until they are heavily textured. Slide a glass bead on one end and, with round-nosed pliers, make a loop at the other end of the wire. Make 14 silver wire jump rings (see page 30).

3 Texture the jump rings by tapping them with a hammer. Thread them through the loops in the bent wire, linking the sections with the flat-nosed pliers. Attach the single wire loop fastener with the remaining jump rings.

SEE ALSO...

* ✳ Coiled loop fastener p.34
* ✳ Coiled hook fastener p.36

Free-form wire brooch

One continuous length of silver wire is decorated with beads and twisted to create an abstract form.

YOU WILL NEED...

* 36 in/90 cm of 14-gauge silver wire

* round-nosed pliers

* eight beads with ¹⁄₃₂-in/0.8 mm hole

* wire cutters

* needle file

* nylon mallet

1 Leaving a ¾-in/2-cm straight piece of wire at the start, begin to curl and bend the remainder of the silver wire into an interesting form.

2 Thread the beads as you go to give an even spread throughout the design.

3 Having produced the final design, curl back the remaining wire to form the pin and cut to the right length. Use the ¾ in/2 cm of wire at the opposite side of the brooch to make a safety hook.

4 File a fine point for the pin, then gently hammer the pin with the nylon mallet.

SEE ALSO...

* Hammering p.26
* Bead wires p.31

Pearl stick pin

The classic combination of fine silver wire
and lustrous pearls creates a dynamic pin
inspired by natural forms.

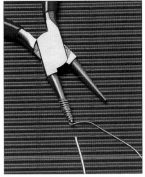

1 Bind the 7-gauge silver wire tightly around one point of the round-nosed pliers to form a cone shape.

2 Take the cone and, using the rest of the wire, bind the cone tightly onto the 14-gauge wire until it is secure. Cut off any excess.

3 Fill the cone of 7-gauge wire with resin-based glue. Push the pearls into the cone and allow the glue to set.

4 Curl and twist the pearls to create an interesting arrangement. Cut and file the pin to a fine point. Place a pin stopper at the end.

YOU WILL NEED...

* 6 in/15 cm of 7-gauge silver wire
* round-nosed pliers
* 5 in/13 cm of 14-gauge silver wire
* wire cutters
* resin-based glue
* eight imitation teardrop pearls on stems
* needle file
* pin stopper

Moon and stars brooch

This magical pin, inspired by the night sky, is formed from loops of chain with a crisp moon and stars motif.

SEE ALSO...

* ✳ Findings p.12

1 Take 4 in/10 cm of the silver wire and fold it in half, curling it over in the center to create a simple spring. Thread half the wire through the tube, leaving half outside to form the pin. Use the excess wire on the other end to form the safety hook.

2 Take 2¾ in/7 cm of the remaining silver wire, thread a silver bead onto the end, loop, then thread this length of wire through the tube. Thread the second bead onto the wire where it protrudes from the tube. Loop and cut off the excess wire.

3 Open the loops of wire at the ends of the tube. Thread the chains onto the loops. Push the loops tightly together so the chains are secure. File any rough edges.

4 Take three ¾-in/2-cm lengths of the remaining silver wire and loop the stars and moon onto the separate lengths. Thread a gold bead onto each length, and loop all three onto the chains.

Chain mail

This chunky bracelet is easy to make, yet will last a lifetime—so why not make it from your favorite precious metal?

1 Simply line three jump rings next to one another as shown. The jump rings become the links in this bracelet.

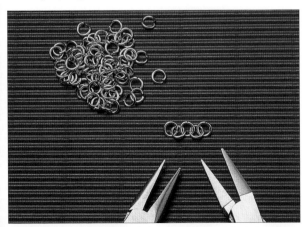

2 Thread a jump ring through two neighboring links to join them, then close with pliers. Repeat until you have five uniform links.

YOU WILL NEED...

* lots and lots of jump rings; the quantity required depends on the size of the rings— you can always make more (see page 30)

* two pairs flat-nosed pliers

* pipe cleaner

* two fasteners

SEE ALSO...

* Findings p.12
* Jump rings p.30

3 Link three jump rings onto the second and fourth link of the five-link chain, as shown. When placed onto a flat surface, they should lie parallel to the first row of rings.

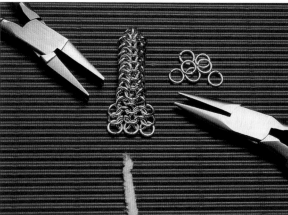

4 Repeat the process in Steps 2 and 3, and continue in this manner until the bracelet is about 3 in/7.5 cm long.

5 The formation of the links should appear very uniform and the bracelet be very flexible. Place the bracelet on a flat surface.

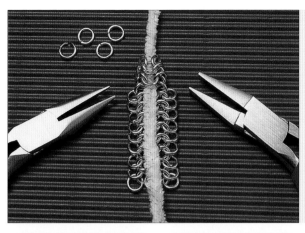

6 At this stage, you will find a pipe cleaner very useful! Keep a close eye on following the pattern you are making with the rings. Put a jump ring through the top two side links and insert the pipe cleaner. Take a second jump ring and thread it through the first, laying it flat on the pipe cleaner. Thread it through the same two side links as above. Close the jump ring with your flat-nosed pliers.

7 Repeat the process of connecting a jump ring to the flat link above it, and then to the two side links. The joins should look uniform and appear the same as the rest of the rings in the bracelet. Continue until you can wrap the bracelet comfortably around your wrist.

8 Add a jump ring and a fastener at either end to complete the bracelet.

Clock piece

Got a broken clock or an old watch lying around? Reconstitute their mechanisms to make this beautiful and unusual brooch.

YOU WILL NEED...

* clock and watch pieces

* resin-based glue

* half-round pliers

* wire cutters

* 2 in/5 cm of 14-gauge silver wire

1 Select some interesting pieces of watch mechanisms and assemble them in an attractive form, making sure that the piece at the end has a hole in it for attaching the hook. Glue together and allow to set.

2 Cut out a small piece from a wheel, leaving most of the circle intact, curl it to make a hook shape, and glue it into the hole in the end section of the completed design. Take a length of clock spring and glue this to the opposite end.

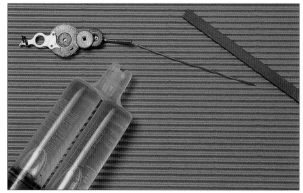

3 Glue the piece of silver wire into the spring and allow to set. Cut the wire to fit along the back of the brooch so it reaches the hook. File to a fine point. The spring keeps the pin under tension.

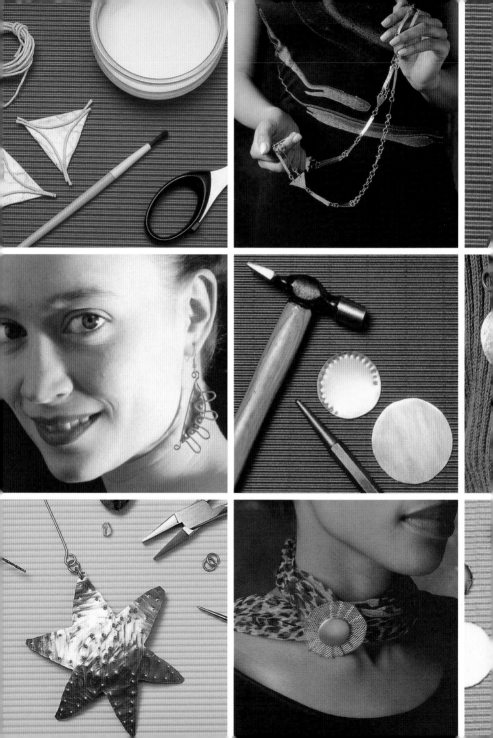

Metal, plastic, and paper

Copper star pendant

Simple techniques are used to add texture to sheet metal, which is then combined with glass beads to create this bold, fun pendant.

YOU WILL NEED...

* marker pen
* 3½ x 3½-in/8.5 x 8.5-cm piece of thin copper sheet metal
* tin snips
* protective gloves
* needle file
* center punch
* hammer
* hand drill
* round-nosed pliers
* flat-nosed pliers
* three glass beads
* two copper jump rings
* bead wire
* 34 in/90 cm of black leather thong

SEE ALSO...

* Hammering p.26
* Bead wires p.31
* Jump rings p.30
* Cutting shapes p.29

1 Draw a star shape on the copper sheet and then cut it out with the tin snips. Make sure you wear a pair of gloves when cutting the metal to protect your hands from the metal's sharp edges.

2 File the star and tap the surface with a hammer to create texture. Place the shape on a wooden surface. Using a center punch and a hammer, tap the back of the star to create a raised pattern.

3 Drill a hole in one of the points of the star. Open up a jump ring, slide it through the hole, and then close it. Use another jump ring to attach the star's jump ring to a bead wire.

4 Slide the beads onto the wire and make a loop with the round-nosed pliers to secure. Fasten the thong around the loop and knot the two ends together to secure.

Rosette button brooch

A button cover is used to hold folded aluminum gauze to fashion a delicate, rosette effect.

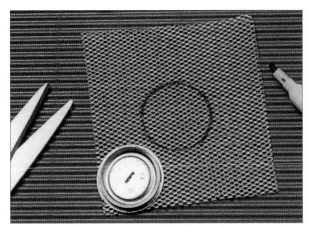

1 Draw around the back of the button cover on the center of the aluminum gauze.

2 Cut out this marked center using scissors. Then, cut away the outside corners to make a more circular shape.

YOU WILL NEED...

* marker pen
* 1-in/2.5-cm metal button
* button cover
* 3-in/7.5-cm square of aluminum gauze
* scissors
* gold spray paint
* round-nosed pliers
* half-round pliers
* flat-nosed pliers
* gold pen
* brooch back
* bead wire
* resin-based glue

SEE ALSO...

* Findings p.12

3 Spray the outside of the button cover with gold paint, following the manufacturer's instructions.

4 Overlap the gauze to make sure that the hole is the right size to fit in the button cover. Trap the gauze inside the cover.

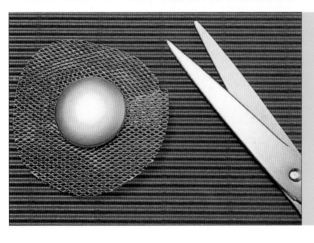

5 Using scissors, cut the gauze into an even shape.

6 Roll over the outer edges of the gauze with the round-nosed pliers to make them durable and safe for skin and clothing. Then, make the edges flat by pressing them with the half-round pliers.

7 Use the half-round pliers to slightly pleat the gauze to make a frill. Using the gold pen, draw a border around the edge.

8 Glue on the brooch back with the resin-based glue.

Celtic-style pin

This imaginative hammer-textured brass and copper pin is inspired by the distinctive art of the ancient Celts.

YOU WILL NEED...

✳ one 3 x 2-in/7.5 x 5-cm piece of thin brass sheet, and one 3 x 2-in/7.5 x 5-cm piece of thin copper sheet

✳ wire wool

✳ pen

✳ paper

✳ resin-based glue

✳ scissors

✳ piercing saw and size 0 saw blade

✳ needle file

✳ chasing hammer

✳ round-nosed pliers

✳ 4¾ in/12 cm of 18-gauge copper wire

✳ decorative bead with ¹⁄₁₆-in/1.5-mm hole

SEE ALSO...

✳ Sawing metal p.28

1 Clean the metal with wire wool. Draw two spiral shapes onto paper and then lightly glue one onto the copper sheet and one onto the brass sheet.

2 Saw-pierce the shapes out of the metal sheets, following your paper template and cutting through the paper at the same time. Remove the paper and then file the rough edges of the metal spirals.

3 Use the chasing hammer to create a textured effect on the copper and brass spirals by hammering the flat metal.

4 Interlock the two spirals to create a pattern. Bend back the outside edge spirals so that the center of the piece arches slightly. Use a little resin glue at the back to hold the pieces in place.

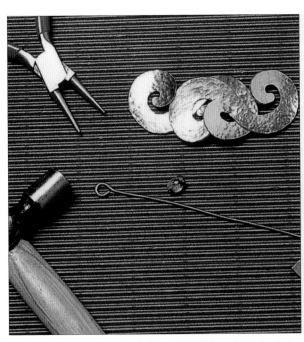

5 Curl the top of the copper wire to form a loop and hammer it flat. Thread on the bead so it is close to the loop. File the other end of the copper wire to a fine point.

6 Thread the wire in through the top spiral and out again through the bottom. This will attach the pin securely to the garment.

Enameled brooch

Enamel paints are used to create bright contrasting—or complementary—colors on a metal surface.

YOU WILL NEED...

* marker pen
* cardboard
* scissors
* paper
* 3¼ x 3¼ in/8.25 x 8.25 cm of thin copper sheet
* wire wool
* tin snips
* piercing saw
* center punch
* nylon mallet
* round-nosed pliers
* 5 in/13 cm of 14-gauge silver wire
* half-round pliers
* wire cutters
* needle file
* paintbrush
* orange and turquoise enamel paints

SEE ALSO...

* Hammering p.26
* Sawing metal p.28
* Cutting shapes p.29

1 Clean the copper with wire wool. On the cardboard, draw a template for a 2½-in/6-cm diameter disc with tabs. Use this to mark the shape onto the copper. Cut out using tin snips.

2 Using the saw, cut a 1½-in/4-cm diameter circle from the center of the copper disc.

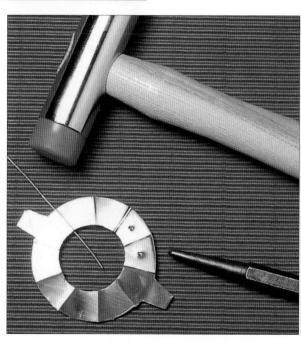

3 Hammer the disc with the nylon mallet over the wire to make indentations in a regular pattern around the brooch. Intersperse with center-punch marks on the back to make a pattern.

4 With the round-nosed pliers, roll one of the tabs over to the back to make a tiny tube. Fold the second tab over and gently curl down its corners. Thread the wire through the tube and fold it back over the tube with the half round pliers to secure it in place. Bend the longer length of the wire to fit across the back of the brooch. Cut to size to enable it to hook under the tab. File to a fine point.

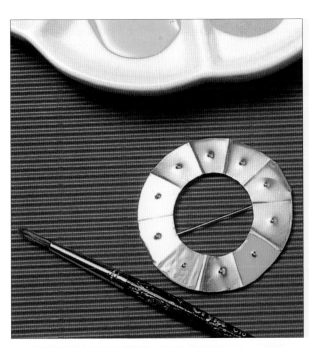

5 Use the enamel paints to color the sections of the brooch. These will give the brooch extra definition and sparkle. Do not paint over the edges. If necessary, lightly clean the raised ridges and center-punch marks to highlight the copper, using the wire wool.

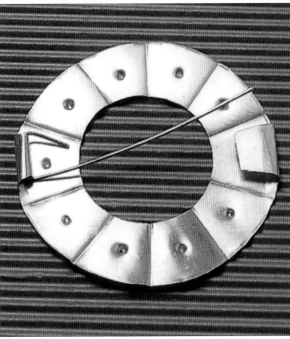

6 When the paint is dry, clean the back of the brooch and file away any rough edges.

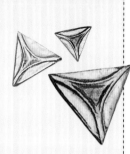

Gilded triangles

These glamorous golden earrings are made from inexpensive and recycled materials. String is used to create a raised surface pattern.

YOU WILL NEED...

* pen
* 4 x 2-in/10 x 5-cm thick cardboard
* scissors
* scrap paper
* PVA glue or wallpaper adhesive
* paintbrush
* 12 in/30 cm of string
* gold foil-type wrapping paper or candy wrapper
* blue foil-type wrapping paper or candy wrapper
* clear varnish
* earring stems and backs
* resin-based glue

SEE ALSO...

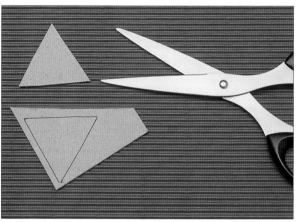

1 Draw and cut out two triangle shapes from cardboard. Keep the edges equal in length and do not make them too large.

2 Cover both sides of the triangles with a layer of torn pieces of paper with PVA or wallpaper paste. Allow to dry for one hour.

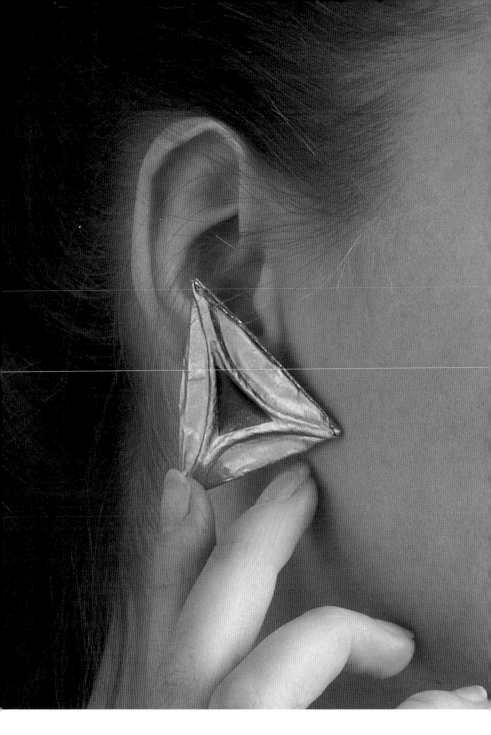

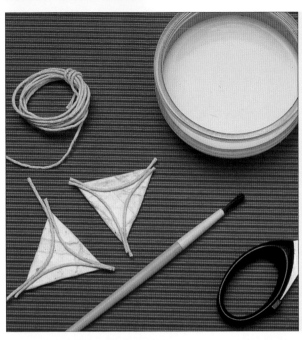

3 Attach three 3-in/7.5-cm lengths of string with glue to the inside edges of both triangles to form an inner triangular pattern. Allow to dry and trim off any excess string.

4 Cover the triangles with glue and place a sheet of gold paper on top of each. Carefully smooth down the paper to define the surface pattern. Fold the gold paper around the triangles to cover the backs and trim off any excess paper if necessary.

5 Cut a small triangle of blue paper foil and glue into the center of each triangle. Following the manufacturer's directions, apply a coat of clear varnish all over the triangles in a well-ventilated area. Allow to dry for six hours.

6 Attach earring stems to the backs of the earrings with resin-based glue to complete them.

Golden fan

A color photocopy on an acetate surface gives strength and durability and creates an easy-to-make and attractive piece of jewelry.

YOU WILL NEED...

* ruler
* 8½ x 11-in/21 x 28-cm color copy of an interesting design on acetate
* scissors
* 8½ x 11-in/21 x 28 cm sheet of white paper
* 6 in/15 cm of 7-gauge silver wire
* ⅛-in/3-mm silver-plated bead
* flat-nosed pliers
* wire cutters
* needle file
* 3½ in/9 cm of 14-gauge nickel wire
* resin-based glue
* pin stopper

1 Cut a strip of acetate 8 in/20 cm long by 1 in/2.5 cm wide. Cut the strip in half to make two 4-in/10-cm strips.

2 Sandwich a strip of 3¾ x ¾-in/9.5 x 2-cm paper between the two acetate strips to allow a border all around. Fold them to form an accordion.

3 Use the fine silver wire to bind the accordion together at one end. Thread on the silver-plated bead and secure by squeezing the wire flat with the flat-nosed pliers. Cut off the excess.

4 Open the other end of the accordion to form a fan. File a point on the nickel wire and, using the resin-based glue, stick it inside the bottom of the fan. Allow to dry. Use silver wire to bind around the base of the fan and down the pin. Put on the pin stopper.

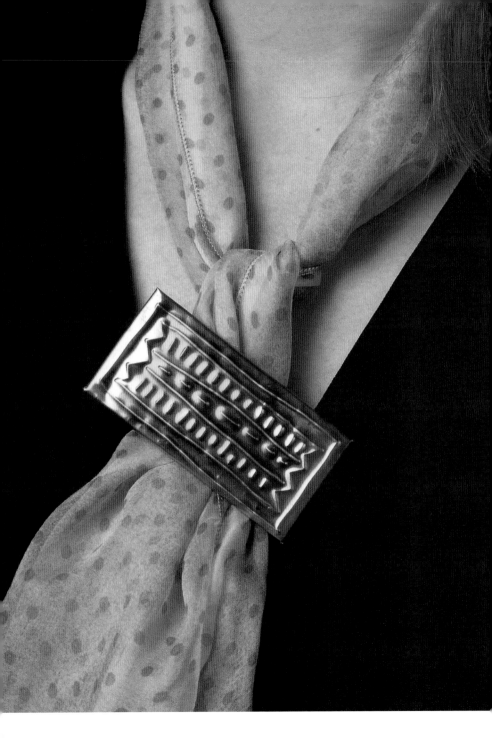

Embossed copper brooch

This is a copper foil brooch with a hand-drawn motif, using gentle heat to color.

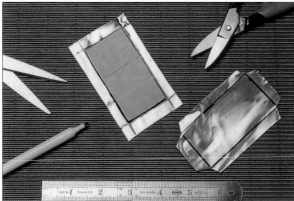

1 Using the cardboard template, draw a 1½ x 3 in/4 x 8 cm rectangle onto the copper foil, extending the lines to the edges. Cut away the corners of the copper to the edge of the template.

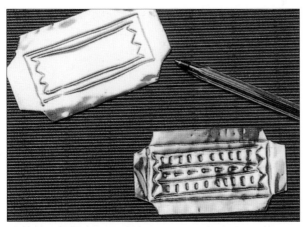

2 Using a ballpoint pen, draw a pattern on the surface of the copper foil. You will need to press quite hard.

YOU WILL NEED...

* marker pen
* ruler
* tin snips
* 3½ x 2 in/9 x 5 cm of copper foil
* ballpoint pen
* flat-nosed pliers
* gas flame
* 1½ x 3 in/4 x 8 cm of cardboard
* scissors
* PVA glue
* 1¼ x 2¾ in/3 x 7 cm of felt
* resin-based glue
* brooch back

SEE ALSO...

* Findings p.12

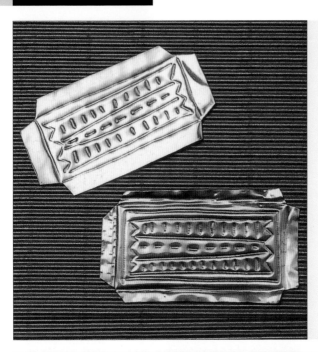

3 Using flat-nosed pliers, hold the copper sheet over a very gentle flame (a gas stove will do.) Keep taking the metal to and from the heat until the metal changes color. Allow the metal to cool before touching it.

4 Place the rectangle of cardboard on the back of the cooled metal and fold the copper edges around the card to secure it.

5 Use PVA glue to stick the felt to the back of the card and over the copper edges.

6 Finally, use the resin-based glue to attach a brooch back to the felt.

Precious stone brooch

Use punching to create pattern and texture around a simply constructed setting for a beautiful stone.

YOU WILL NEED...

* marker pen
* 5 x 4 in/10 x 12.5 cm of cardboard
* scissors
* 2 x 2-in/5 x 5-cm thick aluminum sheet
* 1¾ x 1¾-in/4.5 x 4.5-cm thin brass sheet
* wire wool
* tin snips
* protective gloves
* center punch
* hammer
* ½-in/1-cm diameter flat-back glass stone
* resin-based glue
* brooch back

SEE ALSO...

* Findings p.12
* Cabochon and faceted glass stones p.13
* Hammering p.26

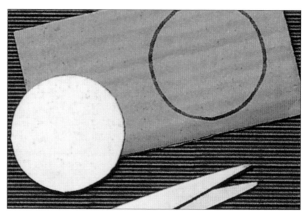

1 Cut out a 2-in/5-cm diameter circle and 1¾-in/4.5-cm diameter circle from the cardboard.

2 Clean the metal with the wire wool. Use the templates to mark the circles on the metal, the larger onto the aluminum, the smaller onto the brass. Cut the circles out of the metal using the tin snips. Wear gloves to protect your hands from the edges.

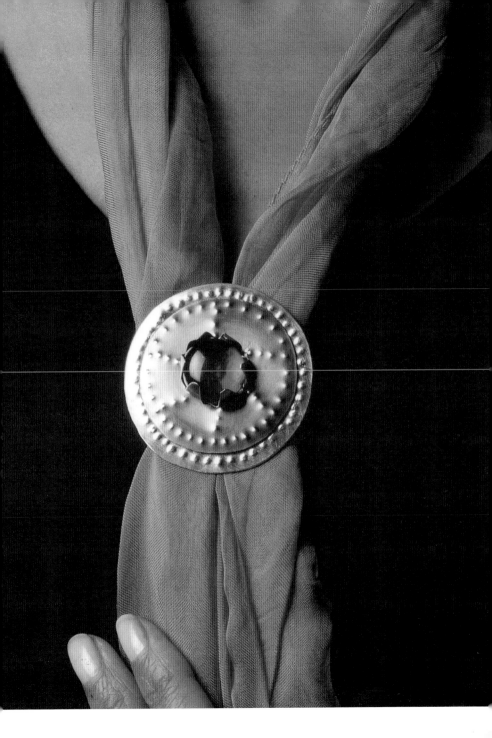

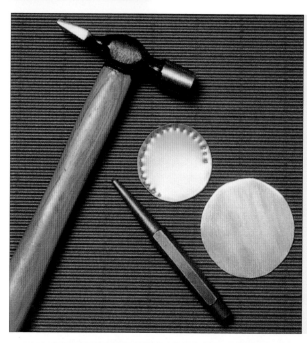

3 Use the center punch to create an indented pattern around the edge of both circles and lines coming in to the center of the brass circle (three punch marks for each line should be enough).

4 Place your stone onto the brass sheet and draw a six-point star around it. Each point should be about ⅜ in/1 cm from the edge of the stone. Cut out the star with snips, taking care not to cut yourself on the sharp edges.

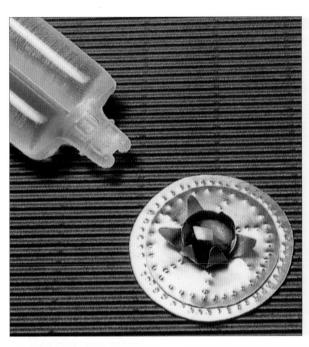

5 Use the resin-based glue to join the aluminum and brass circles together. Wrap the points of the brass star around the stone, which should hold it in place. Glue the stone in its setting to the center of the brass circle and allow the glue to set.

6 Finally, clean the back of the brooch with the wire wool and use resin-based glue to attach the brooch back.

Chain-linked brooch

Colorful plasticized material is linked by delicate chains and bells to make an unusual double-sided brooch.

YOU WILL NEED...

✳ scissors

✳ two different color sticks of modeling plastic

✳ gas flame

✳ six silver-plated bells

✳ drill and ¹⁄₁₆-in/1.5-mm drill bit

✳ flat-nosed pliers

✳ half-round pliers

✳ three lengths of 3½-in/9-cm silver-plated chain

✳ two silver jump rings

✳ resin-based glue

✳ two round brooch backs

SEE ALSO...

✳ Findings p.12
✳ Drilling p.27
✳ Jump rings p.30

1 Cut out two half-circles from one of the modeling plastics. Cut small pieces from the other plastic, lay them on the half-circles, and heat the plastics gently with a flame until they melt together.

2 Drill holes at the top of each semi-circle's arc. Then thread two bells onto each length of chain.

3 Loop the jump rings through the holes in the two half-circles. Lay the chains between them and hook them onto the jump rings. Close the rings to secure the chains.

4 Turn the pieces over and glue one brooch back to each semi-circle, using the resin-based glue.

Brass and glass domes

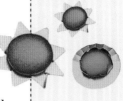

These stunning earrings use a glass dome
for the "stone" setting—and you can vary the
patterned base plate to your own design.

1 Draw around your domed beads with a pen onto the brass
sheet. Sketch a star shape of about eight points around each
circle, depending upon the size of your dome. These will form the
claws to hold your stone in place.

2 Cut out the two stars with tin snips. Remove the very ends of
the points so that they are not dangerously sharp.

YOU WILL NEED...

* marker pen
* two glass domed beads
* 6 x 2-in/15 x 5-cm thin brass sheet
* tin snips
* resin-based glue
* flat needle file
* wire wool
* two earring clip findings, or stems and backs
* metal scriber

SEE ALSO...

* Findings p.12
* Cabochon and faceted glass stones p.13

3 Place a small amount of the resin-based glue in the center of the stars and put the glass domes in position. Leave to dry for 20 minutes.

4 When the adhesive has set, bend the points of the stars to enclose the domes.

5 Draw two 1½-in/4-cm diameter circles onto the remaining brass sheet. Cut out with tin snips.

6 File the edges and clean the metal surface with wire wool. Draw lines ½ in/1 cm long all around the edge of each circle with the metal scriber.

7 Glue the stone setting to the center of the base circle with resin-based glue. Leave to set until fully hardened.

8 Attach an earring clip fitting or posts for pierced ears to the back of each base plate with resin-based glue.

Copper leaves

Combine a thin copper sheet with wire to produce intriguing leafy earrings.

YOU WILL NEED...

* scissors
* cardstock
* gas flame
* six silver-plated bells
* drill and ¹⁄₁₆-in/1.5-mm drill bit
* flat-nosed pliers
* half-round pliers
* three lengths of 3½-in/9-cm silver-plated chain
* two silver jump rings
* resin-based glue
* two round brooch backs
* metal scriber
* copper wire
* nylon mallet

SEE ALSO...

* Hammering p.26
* Drilling p.27
* Findings p.12

1 Cut out a leaf shape template from the cardstock. Draw around it with a metal scriber or pen onto the copper sheet twice.

2 Using tin snips, cut out the two leaf shapes.

3 Using a drill and a small bit, drill a small hole into the top and bottom points of each of the leaf shapes.

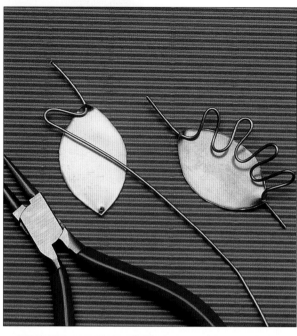

4 Cut two 6½-in/16.5-cm lengths of copper wire. Insert one end of one piece of the wire into each leaf, leaving 1 in/2.5 cm protruding from the top. Using round-nosed pliers, form a zigzag pattern with the wire. Push the other end of the wire through the remaining hole. Repeat the process with the second leaf and wire.

5 Place a ruler (or straight edge) across the leaf as a guide and fold in half with the wire pattern remaining on the outside of the leaf. Repeat with the second leaf.

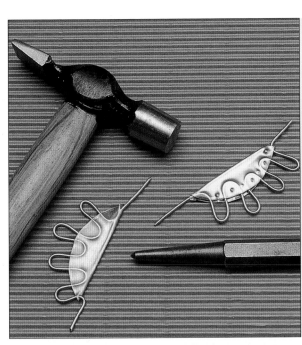

6 Using a center punch and hammer, punch dots between the wire pattern. Next gently hammer the metal surface with a nylon mallet to define the patterns.

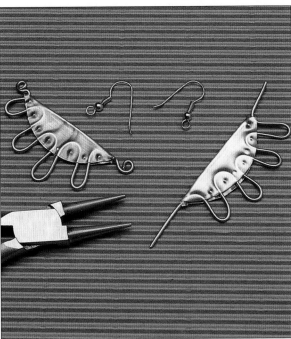

7 Form a spiral using round-nosed pliers on the ends of the wire. Attach earring hooks to the top spiral to complete.

Bird and flower drops

Here, intricate saw-pierced motifs are linked together. A single motif could be used to make smaller, dainty earrings.

1 Draw bird, flower, and heart shapes onto the card, then cut out to form templates.

2 Cover the pieces of silver and brass sheet with masking tape.

3 Use the templates to draw: two birds and two flowers on the silver sheet; two hearts and two flowers on the brass sheet.

4 Drill large center holes into the flowers. Remember to center punch before attempting to drill any holes. Next, drill small holes at the top and bottom of the birds, hearts, and silver flowers. The remaining brass flowers require only one hole at the top.

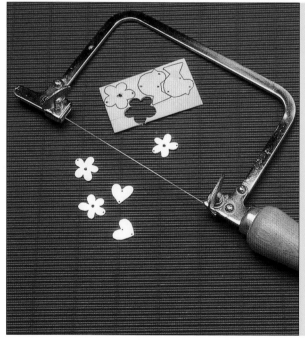

5 Saw-pierce the shapes from the metal sheets.

6 Remove the masking tape and file the edges. Clean the metal surface with wire wool to bring up the shine.

7 Link the shapes together with jump rings through the drilled holes and attach earring hooks to finish.

Silvery circles

Combine metal with fabric—perhaps to match a favorite outfit. Hammered sheet aluminum is an alternative to textured aluminum.

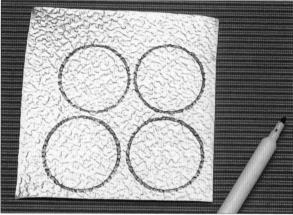

1 Draw two 1½-in/4-cm and two 1¼-in/3-cm diameter circles on the aluminum sheet with the compass.

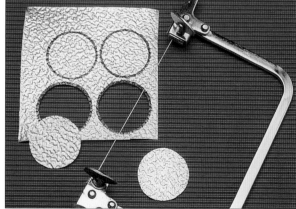

2 Using a piercing saw, cut out all four of the aluminum circles, and lay them flat on the work surface.

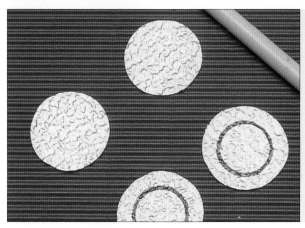

3 Draw 1-in/2.5-cm diameter circles in the center of the larger circles.

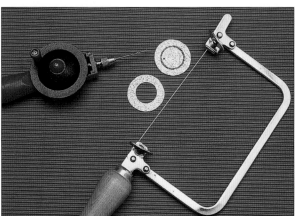

4 Drill a small hole near the edge of the inner circle, insert the saw blade, and pierce out the centers of both the larger circles.

5 Smooth both edges of the larger circles using files and emery paper.

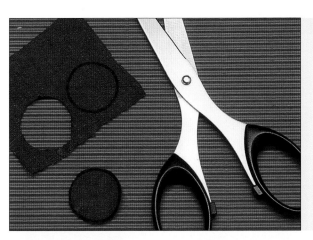

6 Cut out two 1¼-in/3-cm diameter circles of fabric.

7 Put a tiny ball of stuffing into the center of each fabric circle and apply a small amount of clear adhesive or PVA to secure in place. Put the fabric on top of the circle with the center removed.

8 Glue on the backing circle of aluminum with resin-based glue, thus sandwiching the fabric between the two metal discs. Hold together with clips until the glue has set. Attach stem fittings to the backs to finish the earrings.

Textured brass

Bold geometric shapes are assembled in a strong pattern to fashion a necklace that has echoes of ancient Mexican civilizations.

YOU WILL NEED...

* ✳ ruler
* ✳ pen
* ✳ 4 x 4 in/10 x 10 cm of brass sheet
* ✳ protective gloves
* ✳ tin snips
* ✳ hammer
* ✳ needle file
* ✳ center punch
* ✳ hand drill and $\frac{1}{32}$-in/0.8-mm drill bit
* ✳ 110 in/280 cm of 14-gauge brass wire
* ✳ two pairs of flat-nosed pliers
* ✳ round-nosed pliers

SEE ALSO...

* ✳ Hammering p.26
* ✳ Jump rings p.30

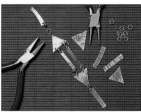

1 Draw ten triangles of $\frac{7}{8}$ x $\frac{7}{8}$ in/2 x 2 cm and also 13 rectangles of 1$\frac{1}{8}$ x $\frac{1}{4}$ in/3 x 0.5 cm on the brass sheet. Wearing protective gloves, use the tin snips to cut out the drawn shapes. Gently tap the surface of the metal shapes with a hammer until they are textured all over.

2 File the edges of the metal shapes. With a center punch, mark drill positions, three holes on the triangles and two holes on the rectangles. With a hand drill, make the necessary holes. Make 109 jump rings (see page 30).

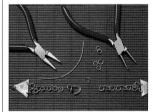

3 With two pairs of flat-nosed pliers, open the jump rings and, one by one, slip them through the holes drilled in the metal shapes. Close the jump rings. Lay out the shapes in the sequence shown and attach the components, making sure there are three jump rings between each metal shape.

4 To finish the ends of the necklace, make a chain by linking together 14 jump rings using two pairs of flat-nosed pliers, then attach a brass coiled loop (see page 34) and hook fastener (see page 36).

Cupid earrings

For these earrings, you can also use designs such as ballet dancers or golden slippers with corresponding saw-pierced shapes.

1 Using a piercing saw, remove the stem at the back of the cupid cake decorations and discard.

2 Draw two small hearts onto the aluminum sheet. Ensure that these are in scale with the Cupids and are not too large.

YOU WILL NEED...

* two plastic cupid cake decorations
* piercing saw frame and 2/0 saw blades
* 1 x 1-in/2.5 cm x 2.5-cm aluminum sheet
* resin-based glue
* center punch
* drill
* emery paper
* red and gray enamel paint
* two jump rings
* round-nosed pliers
* two earring hooks

SEE ALSO...

* Findings p.12
* Drilling p.27
* Sawing metal p.28
* Jump rings p.30

3 Cut out the two hearts with the piercing saw.

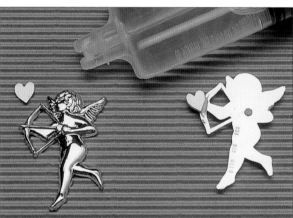

4 Use resin-based glue to glue the hearts to the cupids. Allow to set.

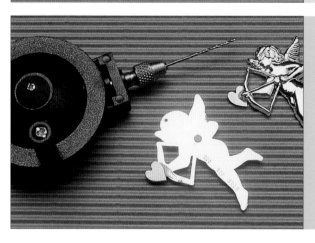

5 Mark with a center punch and drill a small hole through the top of each cupid.

6 Remove some of the silver coating from the surface of the cupid with emery paper.

7 Paint the clean surface with gray enamel paint and the heart with red. Allow to dry.

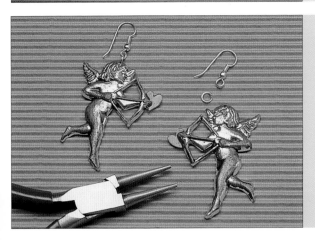

8 Attach a jump ring with round-nosed pliers and an earring hook to each earring.

Beads, shells, and stones

Shells and pearls

Seashore finds can be transformed into exotic creations. Shells are often surprisingly robust and will prove durable as earrings.

1 Select similar shells to incorporate into your earrings. Drill a small hole through each shell. To prevent splitting, drill through the central part of the shell.

2 Paint the shells with a clear varnish in a well-ventilated area. This gives them a sheen and a better appearance. Allow to dry. Meanwhile cut two 4-in/10-cm lengths of wire.

3 Form a small spiral on one end of one wire. Thread on a shell, a pearl, two shells, another pearl, two more shells, and a final pearl. Repeat this process with the other wire.

4 Form another spiral at the end of each earring wire. Fit an earring hook to the spiral on each earring to complete.

Bead and tube necklace

Extruded rubber tube is used in striking contrast with large, bright beads to create a highly tactile and modern necklace.

YOU WILL NEED...

* craft knife

* 24 in/60 cm of 11-gauge black rubber tube

* 30 in/76 cm of black leather thong

* scissors

* fourteen varied glass beads

1 With a craft knife, cut the rubber tube into 13 sections measuring 1½ in/4 cm in length.

2 Tie a knot in one end of the thong. Thread the tubes and beads onto the leather thong in the order shown.

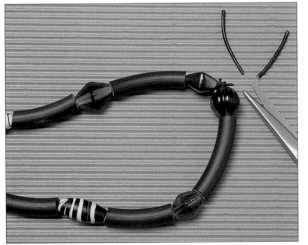

3 When all of the components are threaded, tie a knot in the other end of the leather thong and trim the ends using scissors.

SEE ALSO...

* Fastener for leather thong p.33

Natural necklace

Earth-toned ceramic beads are widely spaced on a linen thread to create a simple, natural effect.

YOU WILL NEED...

* scissors

* 2½ yards/2.3 meters of thick linen thread

* ruler

* twelve natural ceramic beads

1 With the scissors, cut two lengths of linen thread measuring 45 in/115 cm each. Place one end of each length together, and tie in a knot, about 2½ in/7.5 cm from the end of each piece of thread.

2 Slide a ceramic bead onto the threads until it rests on the knot. Tie another knot on the other side of the bead, securing it in place. Measure 2 in/5 cm from the bead, and tie another knot. Slide on another bead and secure this with a knot. Repeat this process until all the beads are used.

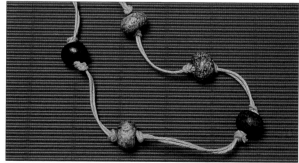

3 To finish the necklace, tie the ends of the threads together next to a bead so that the fastening is discreetly covered.

Seashell choker

Found natural forms provide inspiration for this necklace, which combines small seashells, beads, and braided linen thread.

1 Cut the natural linen thread into six 15-in/38-cm lengths. Separate the linen threads into two piles of three thread lengths.

2 Glue the ends of the three threads together and leave to dry. Braid each pile of three threads and glue to secure at the other end. Leave to dry.

3 Sew the two braided lengths together at one end, then sew on the shells and beads in a random fashion. Sew the other ends of the braided lengths together.

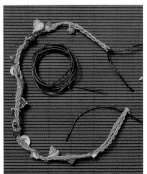

4 Cut two 8-in/20-cm lengths of leather thong. Thread one thong through one end of the braided lengths, and the other thong through the other end. Tie a knot to secure each.

YOU WILL NEED...

* 2½ yards/2.3 meters of of thick linen thread
* scissors
* glue
* needle and thread
* sixteen small mixed seashell beads
* five small glass beads
* 16 in/40 cm of black leather thong

SEE ALSO...

* Findings p.12

Chunky bead choker

Hundreds of brightly colored glass beads are strung in quantities, and combined to produce a chunky necklace design.

YOU WILL NEED...

* wire snips

* 4½ yards/4 meters of 14-gauge copper wire

* round-nosed pliers

* 162 glass beads in an assortment of colors, shapes, and sizes

* 20 in/50 cm of black leather thong

* 29 glass beads, all of the same type (spacer beads)

* flat-nosed pliers

SEE ALSO...

* Bead wires p.31
* Coiled loop fastener p.34
* Coiled hook fastener p.36

1 With the wire snips, cut 54 pieces of wire about 2½ in/7.5 cm long. (The length of the cut wires may vary depending on the size of the beads used.)

2 Secure one end of the wire with the round-nosed pliers and carefully bend the wire to create a loop at the end.

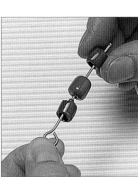

3 Thread three assorted beads onto the wire.

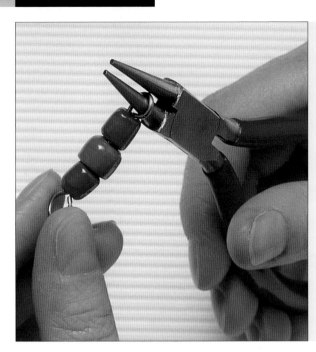

4 With the round-nosed pliers, make another loop in the other end of the wire to secure the beads.

5 Repeat steps 3 and 4 until you have made another 53 beaded wires.

6 Thread the leather thong through one of the loops in the beaded wire. Interspace each series of beaded wires with a spacer bead threaded directly onto the thong at regular intervals, as shown. Repeat the threading and spacer beads until all of the beaded wires have been used.

7 When all the component beaded wires have been used, thread 12 spacer beads onto the thong at each end of the mass of beaded wires. Attach a coiled loop (see page 34) and hook fastener (see page 36) to the ends of the thong, then tie a knot in the ends of the thong so that the fastening is secure.

Pebble bracelet

It is important that the wire is wrapped around the stones tightly and securely to keep the bracelet together.

YOU WILL NEED...

* ✳ pebbles in various sizes
* ✳ wire cutters
* ✳ 92 in/235 cm of metal wire
* ✳ round-nosed pliers
* ✳ two metal beads for each stone
* ✳ flat-nosed pliers
* ✳ large and small jump rings

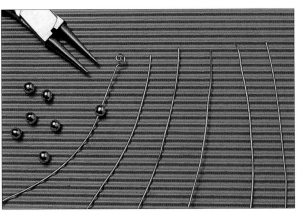

1 The quantity of pebbles used will vary. The sample shown uses six, but your bracelet may use more or less. Cut a length of wire approximately 4 in/10 cm long. Spiral the end, using your round-nosed pliers, and add a small metal bead.

2 Wrap the wire tightly around the pebble, making a small loop on either side when you reach the mid point.

3 Continue securing the pebble within the wire, then twist the two small loops (from Step 2) with your round-nosed pliers.

4 Place a metal bead onto the wire before making a small spiral in the wire. If you have excess wire, trim it with your wire cutters.

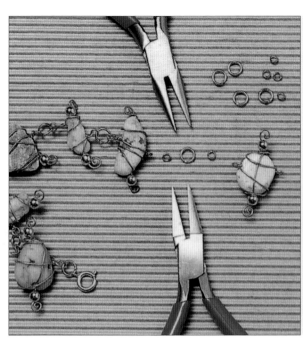

5 Link a small jump ring to the "twisted loop" on either side of the pebble, then pass a larger jump ring through these to link the pebbles together. Add a fastener to the ends of the bracelet.

6 Varnish the bracelet all over in a well-ventilated area and leave overnight to dry.

Coiled brass and beads

The combination of aluminum and large, richly colored glass beads creates a sophisticated, textural neckpiece.

YOU WILL NEED...

* wire snips

* 13½ yards/12.3 meters of 14-gauge brass wire

* round-nosed pliers

* eleven large, colored glass beads

* 40 in/100 cm of black leather thong

* five aluminum beads

* scissors

1 With wire snips, cut 64 7½-in/20-cm lengths of brass wire. Using the round-nosed pliers, coil the lengths of wire to make 64 coiled wire "beads."

2 Thread the glass beads, aluminum beads, and coiled wire beads onto the leather thong in the sequence shown, spacing four coiled beads between each glass or aluminum bead.

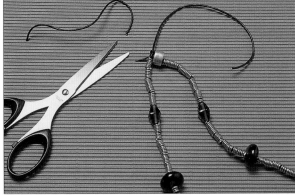

3 To finish, tie the ends of the leather thong together and then trim the ends with a pair of scissors.

SEE ALSO...

* Fastener for thong p.33

Foiled bead choker

Brightly colored foiled glass beads are strung vertically onto a thick, flexible wire choker that is worn close to the neck.

YOU WILL NEED...

* 6 yards/5.5 m of 14-gauge steel wire

* round-nosed pliers

* wire snips

* two pairs flat-nosed pliers

* 150 small foiled glass beads

* clear varnish

* paintbrush

SEE ALSO...

* Jump rings p.30
* Bead wires p.31
* Coiled loop fastener p.34
* Coiled hook fastener p.36

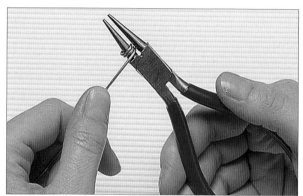

1 Make 132 steel jump rings. Cut 6-in/15-cm lengths of wire, secure one end of each length in a pair of round-nosed pliers and slowly bend the wire around one side of the pliers.

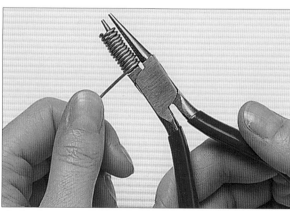

2 Continue to coil the wire around the round-nosed pliers until all of the wire is used and an even coil of wire is formed along the pliers. Make sure that the wire coils are evenly tightened and evenly spaced apart.

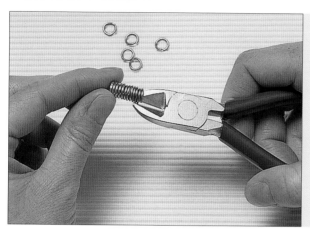

3 Remove the coil from the pliers and, using a pair of wire snips, cut up one side of the coil.

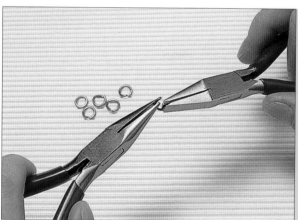

4 To open the jump rings, use two pairs of flat-nosed pliers and twist the ends away from one another. Thread on another jump ring or beaded wire and close up the first jump ring to secure.

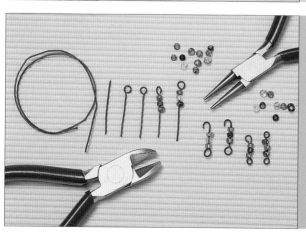

5 With the wire snips, cut 50 1-in/2.5-cm lengths of steel wire. With the round-nosed pliers, make a loop at one end of the wire. Thread three beads onto the wire and make a loop at the other end of the wire to secure the beads and for fastening. Repeat this process with the other 49 wires.

6 Link each beaded wire together using a jump ring. Once the jump ring has been threaded on, use the flat-nosed pliers to make sure it is securely closed. Repeat until all of the beaded wires are linked together with jump rings, as shown.

7 To complete the necklace, make a chain by linking 16 jump rings, using the flat-nosed pliers to open and close the links.

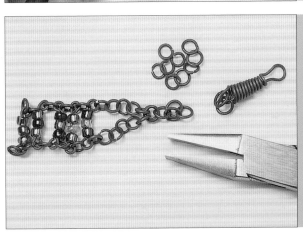

8 The chain joins onto either end of the last beaded wires, and these two chains then come together to become a single longer chain. Then, attach a coiled loop (see page 34) and a hook fastener (see page 36) to the last links on the necklace. To finish, protect the steel wire with a layer of clear varnish applied in a well-ventilated area.

Steely swirls and marbles

Iridescent marbles, wrapped in wire casings, are linked together with loosely coiled sections of wire in this bold necklace.

YOU WILL NEED...

* wire snips

* 6 yards/5.5 meters of 14-gauge galvanized steel wire

* round-nosed pliers

* fourteen flat-backed glass marbles

* wire

1 With wire snips, cut a length of galvanized steel wire 10 in/25 cm long. Using the round-nosed pliers, make a loop in the wire and then wrap the wire around the marble.

2 When the marble is wrapped in wire, make another loop in the end of the wire. These loops connect one section to another. Repeat until all of the marbles are wrapped.

3 To make the connecting spirals. Cut a 5-in/12.5-cm length of wire and loosely wrap it around one side of a pair of round-nosed pliers. Bend the top and bottom loops in half.

4 Link a spiral between every marble section. Join all of the marbles and spirals together securely until they form a necklace.

SEE ALSO...

* Cabochon and faceted glass stones p.13

Mixed media

Springy hearts and beads

To change the theme on this fun piece, try using brightly colored tissue paper instead of wrapping paper—or even recycled paper.

YOU WILL NEED...

* ten pipe cleaners
* wire snips
* colored wrapping paper, cut into thin strips
* strong adhesive
* pen
* 3 x ½-in/7.5 x 1-cm thin metal sheet
* metal shears
* emery paper
* 36 in/90 cm of 7-gauge metal wire
* round-nosed pliers
* small drill
* paper varnish
* 18 in/45 cm of elastic and a large needle
* nine glass beads

SEE ALSO...

* Drilling p.27

1 Make a three-dimensional heart-shaped frame from as many pipe cleaners as you need.

2 Cover the heart-shaped frame with strips of colored paper, securing the ends with strong adhesive.

3 Onto your metal sheet, draw a heart shape the same size as the heart-shaped frame you made in Step 1. Cut it out, using your metal shears. Glue the metal heart onto the paper-covered heart.

4 Rub the emery paper on the top of the metal heart, to create an even satin finish to the metal.

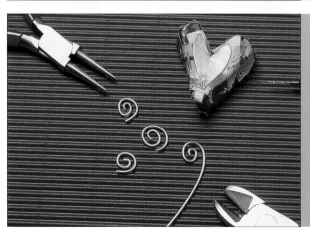

5 Make four metal wire curls, from about 1 in/2.5 cm of wire each. Glue these evenly to the sides of the heart. Drill one hole through the bottom and one hole through the top of the heart, through the centers of the spirals and paper bodies.

6 Repeat Steps 1–5 until you have three complete hearts. Varnish the hearts in a well-ventilated area, and leave overnight to dry.

7 With your round-nosed pliers, make a lot of little wire spirals. These will be threaded onto the elastic between the glass beads.

8 Tie a knot in the end of the elastic and thread it through the holes made in the bottoms of the hearts, the metal spirals, and the beads, as shown. Tie the ends of the elastic together and glue the knot securely. Repeat this step, this time threading the elastic through the holes in the tops of the hearts.

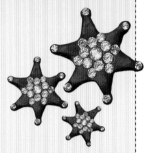

Diamante star brooch

In this glamorous piece, soft moldable material is used to make simple settings for faux diamonds.

YOU WILL NEED...

* thin card
* scissors
* blue modeling clay
* rolling pin
* scalpel
* 1 in/2.5 cm of 14-gauge silver wire
* six ¼-in/5-mm glass diamonds
* 12 ⅛-in/3-mm glass diamonds
* six ¹⁄₁₆-in/1.5-mm glass diamonds
* oven
* needle and thread
* 20 in/50 cm of 1-in/2.5-cm silver ribbon
* brooch back
* resin-based glue

SEE ALSO...

* Findings p.12

1 Cut a star shape out of card. Roll out the clay to a thickness of approximately ¼ in/5 mm. Lay the star template on top and lightly outline it with the scalpel.

2 Cut out the star, allowing a small ball of extra clay at all points of the star (approximately ¼ in/5 mm in diameter). Mold the clay to create a smooth shape.

3 Push some wire through the side of one point of the star to make a hole. Push the glass diamonds into the center of the star and onto its points to form the desired pattern, then remove the glass diamonds, leaving the indentations in the clay. Follow manufacturer's directions to bake the star in the oven to harden it.

4 After the clay has been baked and hardened, stick the glass diamonds back into the star, using the resin-based glue, and allow them to set.

5 Using the silver wire, make a loop through the hole in the star that you made in Step 3. Thread the silver ribbon through this loop and make a bow. Cut off any excess.

6 Sew a brooch back to the back of the bow.

Colorful fossil form

The beautifully evocative shapes of seashells are used to make a mold that produces a fossilized-looking treasure from the deep.

YOU WILL NEED...

* self-hardening clay

* 2 x ¾-in/5 x 2-cm wood block

* assorted small seashells

* plaster of paris

* 2 in/5 cm of wire

* scalpel

* paintbrushes

* blue, green, and gold inks

* 3 in/7.5 cm of embroidery thread

* silver-plated fish bead

* ⅛-in/3-mm blue glass bead

* pin back

* resin-based glue

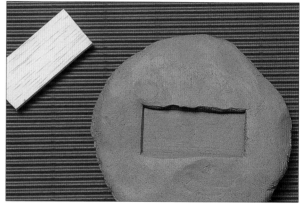

1 Roll out the clay with your hands into a ½-in/1-cm thick slab. Push the wooden block evenly into the clay to make an impression approximately ¼ in/5 mm deep.

2 Use the seashells to make further impressions in the clay within the boundaries of the first impression. Remove the shells, leaving behind their forms and textures.

SEE ALSO...

* Findings p.12

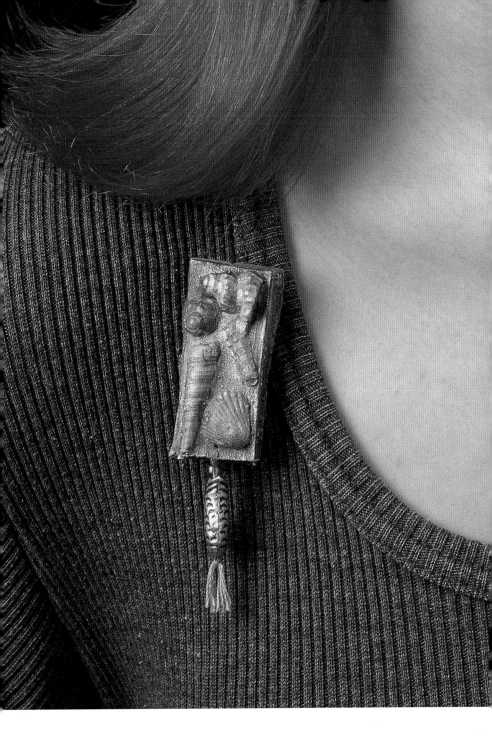

3 Mix the plaster of paris according to instructions and pour it carefully into the mold. Clean away any plaster from the edges.

4 When the plaster has begun to set, push a wire through the thin end of the plaster shape. Move it around slightly to enlarge the hole.

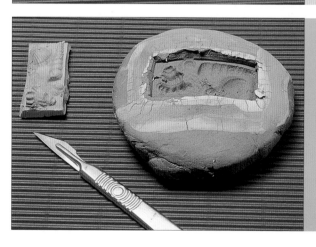

5 When the plaster has set hard, remove it from the clay and leave it to dry completely (until the plaster has become very white; overnight is a good idea.)

6 Paint the plaster form using a mixture of green and blue inks. When these have dried, paint on some gold highlights.

7 Thread the embroidery thread through the hole in the brooch and then thread on the fish and blue glass beads.

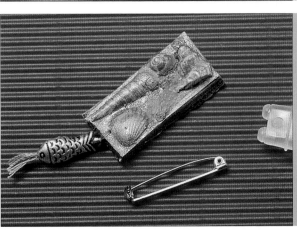

8 Knot the thread to secure it through the brooch. Cut the thread approximately ⅜ in/1 cm below the knot and open the threads to give a tassel effect. Attach the pin back to the back of the plaster form using the resin-based glue. Allow to set.

Bead and leather bracelet

You can change the "earthy" mood shown here by using colorful glass beads or painted ceramic beads from around the world.

YOU WILL NEED...

* 2½ yards/2.3 meters leather thong
* scissors
* hook
* two smaller contrasting ceramic beads
* chunky glass or ceramic beads (quantity depends on the size)
* strong adhesive
* wire cutters

SEE ALSO...

* Single wire loop fastener p. 34
* Single wire hook fastener p. 36

1 Cut one length of leather thong approximately 18 in/45 cm long, fold into two, and tie a small loop knot, as shown. Use the remainder of the leather thong to thread through the knot before securing tightly.

2 Place the loop over the hook and start by threading a smaller bead onto the shorter pair of strands. Tie the outer strands into a bow knot around the bead, once over the top of the inner strands, once below and again above.

3 Repeat Step 2, but with the larger chunky beads. Stop when the bracelet is about 7 in/18 cm long.

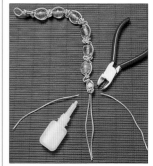

4 Add the second smaller bead, tie the outer strands, and glue into place. Cut remaining outer strands.

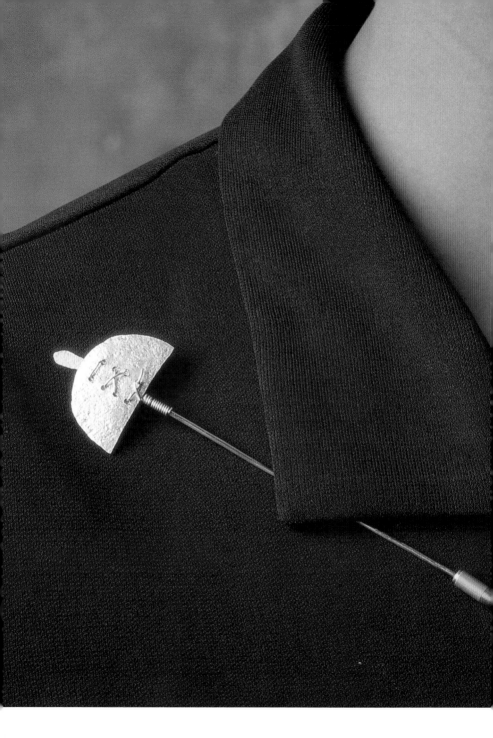

Silver laced stick pin

Create a simple but delightful stick pin using contrasting metals laced together with fine silver wire.

1 Draw a semi-circle on paper, the bottom edge 1 in/2.5 cm long, and the top arc ¾ in/1.5 cm high. Lightly glue to the silver sheet. When dry, cut out and remove the template.

2 Using the chasing hammer, texture the surface of the silver arc. Spread and flatten one end of the brass wire, and file the other end of the wire to a fine point.

3 Lay the flattened brass wire in position across the arc. Drill four 0.5-mm holes into the arc either side of the wire. Using the silver wire, lace the brass wire and arc together.

4 Spiral the leftover silver wire tightly around the thicker brass pin under the silver arc for about ⅜ in/1 cm. Cut off any excess, and put the pin stopper on the end.

YOU WILL NEED...

* pen
* paper
* glue
* 1 x ¾-in/2.5 x 2-cm of thin sheet silver
* tin snips
* chasing hammer
* 4 in/10 cm of 14-gauge brass wire
* 4 in/10 cm of 7-gauge silver wire
* needle file
* half-round pliers
* drill and 0.5-mm drillbit
* wire snips
* pin stopper

SEE ALSO...

* Hammering p.26

Leather and fine copper

Tightly bound strands of leather thong are restrained with fine wire and joined with large jump rings to make an unusual chain.

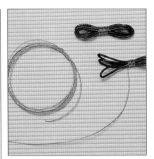

1 With scissors, cut nine equal lengths of black leather thong and wrap one around the piece of cardboard.

2 Cut nine lengths of fine copper wire. Slide the leather thong carefully off the piece of card and bind a length of copper wire around the thong, ensuring the loose ends are tied under the wire. Repeat for the remaining thong pieces.

3 Make 22 jump rings out of the 14-gauge wire. Use three jump rings to link the bundles of thong together, attaching the rings directly around the coiled leather loops.

4 When all of the leather sections have been linked together, make and attach a coiled copper wire loop (see page 34) and hook fastening (see page 36).

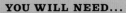

Pearly choker

Creamy mother-of-pearl buttons sewn onto a contrasting black silk ribbon make a simple yet elegant choker.

1 Measure a length of ribbon to fit loosely around the neck. Cut the ribbon and sew the Velcro to each of the ends. Bend the ribbon in half to find the center.

2 Using a needle and thread, sew the first button in the center of the silk ribbon.

YOU WILL NEED...

* 14 in/35 cm of ¾-in/ 1-cm wide black silk ribbon

* scissors

* 1 in/2.5 cm of ⅝-in/1.5-cm Velcro

* needle and black thread

* five mother-of-pearl buttons

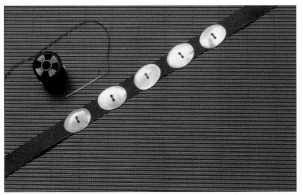

3 Continue to sew the buttons, at even distances from one another, on either side of the center button, until all five buttons have been used.

Silver swirls and stars

Instead of using black acrylic sheet for these earrings, you can use other colored or clear plastic, and copper or brass wire and beads.

YOU WILL NEED...

* cardstock
* 1½ in x 3 in/4 x 7.5 cm of ⅛-in/3-mm black Perspex sheet
* masking tape
* piercing saw frame and 2/0 blades
* emery paper
* flat needle file
* center punch
* drill and ¹⁄₁₆-in/1.5 mm drill bit
* 10 in/25 cm of 14-gauge sterling silver round section wire
* four small silver beads
* wire cutters
* chain-nosed pliers
* hammer
* two earring hooks

SEE ALSO...

* Hammering p.26
* Drilling p.27
* Cutting shapes p.29

1 Make a star template from cardstock. Cover the Perspex sheet with masking tape and use the template to draw two stars.

2 Using the piercing saw frame, saw-pierce the two stars out of the Perspex sheet, and remove the masking tape.

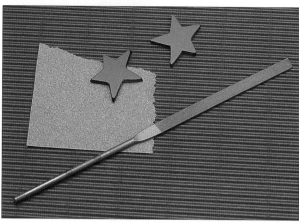

3 File and smooth the edges of the two stars with the emery paper and the flat needle file until all traces of cutting marks are removed.

4 Center-punch the center of each star, then drill a hole through it.

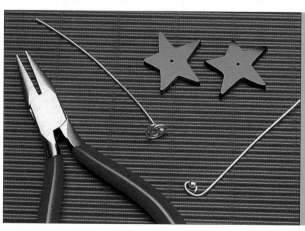

5 Cut two 5-in/12.5-cm lengths of silver wire. Insert a bead onto one end and curl the wire around to prevent the bead from falling off, then form a small spiral around the bead. Repeat this process with the other wire.

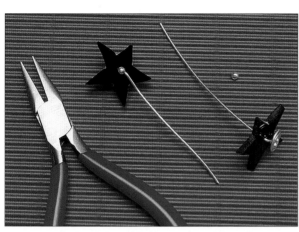

6 Push a wire through the hole in each Perspex star and insert another bead onto the wire. Bend the wire so that it runs flat against the back of the star shape.

7 Form a wavy pattern with the remaining wire and cut to your desired length. Make a small loop at the very end and hammer the wire flat.

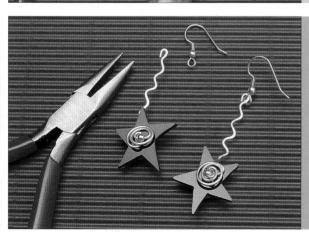

8 Attach earring hooks to the top loops of wire to complete the earrings.

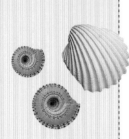

Patterned drop earrings

If you prefer, heat modeling plastic in an oven on low heat instead of in hot water.

YOU WILL NEED...

* ruler

* scissors

* two 1-in/2.5-cm strips of "friendly plastic" or modeling plastic in purple

* four ¾-in/1.5-cm squares of modeling plastic in silver

* hot water

* tweezers

* seashells

* drill and small drill bit or darning needle

* six jump rings

* round-nosed pliers

* resin-based glue

* two earring stems and backs

SEE ALSO...

* Jump rings p.30
* Drilling p.27

1 Place a purple piece and a silver square in hot water until the plastic becomes soft and malleable. Carefully remove the pieces from the water using tweezers, then put the silver square on top of the purple piece. Next, press them onto a shell where the plastic will mold to the texture of the shell. You can remove the plastic right away, and it will become quite hard again after about five minutes. Repeat the process with the other purple and silver pieces.

2 Heat the two remaining silver squares in water and press into a different shell surface, following Step 1.

3 Drill ⅟₃₆-in/0.7-mm holes or push a darning needle through the top of each of the four pieces near the center.

4 Take three jump rings and, using the round-nosed pliers to interlock and seal them, link one smaller square to one larger piece. Repeat this process using the remaining two pieces and three jump rings. To complete the earrings, attach the earring stems to the back of the smaller squares with resin-based glue.

Suppliers

Many craft retailers and chain stores, such as Michaels, A.C. Moore, and Pear Art & Craft Supply, carry jewelry-making products; check the internet and your local phone directory.

EQUIPMENT AND TOOLS SUPPLIERS

✳AllCraft Jewelry Supply
Company Inc.
135 West 29th Street
New York, NY 10001

✳Beadbox
4860 E. Baseline Suite 101
Mesa, Arizona 85206

✳Beadworks
905 South Ann Street
Baltimore, MD 21231

✳Fire Mountain Gems
1 Fire Mountain Way
Grants Pass, OR 97526-2373

✳Helby Import Co.
37 Hayward Avenue
Carteret, NJ 07008
Wholesale to specialty bead
shops

✳Paul H Gesswein's Co Inc.
255 Hancock Avenue
Bridgeport, CT 06605

✳Rings & Things
P.O. Box 450
Spokane, WA 99210-0450

✳Swest Inc.
www.swestinc.com

Index

Colour separation by
Pica Digital, Singapore.
Printed and bound in
China by Midas Printing
International Limited.